Institutions and Leadership:
Prospects for the Future

16 June 1987

*To Mum and Dad
with lots of love —*

Don

THE CREDIBILITY OF INSTITUTIONS, POLICIES AND LEADERSHIP
A Series funded by the Hewlett Foundation
Kenneth W. Thompson, *Series Editor*

Institutions and Leadership: Prospects for the Future

The Credibility of Institutions, Policies and Leadership
Volume 20

Edited by

Kenneth W. Thompson

University Press
of America

Lanham • New York • London

The
White Burkett
Miller Center

University of Virginia

Library of Congress Cataloging in Publication Data

Institutions and leadership.

(The Credibility of institutions, policies and
leadership ; v. 20)
    Bibliography: p.
    1. United States—Foreign relations—1981-
2. United States—Politics and government—1981-
3. Presidents—United States.   I.Thompson, Kenneth W.,
1921-   II. Series.
E876.I57   1986   320.973   86-24668
ISBN 0-8191-5737-6 (alk. paper)
ISBN 0-8191-5738-4 (pbk. : alk. paper)

Dedicated
to
President Roger W. Heyns

Table of Contents

Part IV The Credibility of Leadership in the Future

Preface

The present volume concludes the Hewlett Foundation Series on the credibility of American leadership and institutions. It contains a collection of essays by recognized authorities on one aspect or another of policy and leadership. A few of the contributors are drawn from abroad (Herbert G. Nicholas and Yuen Foong Khong). However these writers are men who have devoted themselves to the careful study of American politics and government.

Most observers are cautious about looking to the future and contributors to this work are no exception. They are hesitant to forecast how trends will work themselves out in the face of all the contingent elements of history. Nonetheless, the main authors in this study make clear where they consider certain trends and tendencies are leading. In so doing, they help us look to the future.

Introduction

No study of leadership and policy in the future can be stronger than those who undertake the inquiry. Fortunately, the papers assembled in Volume XX of the Hewlett Foundation Series include papers by some of the most thoughtful observers in the English speaking world.

Herbert G. Nicholas of Oxford University in England has written widely on American and world politics. No book is more important than *The Nature of American Politics*. He has also been the teacher and mentor of American Rhodes Scholars who have gone on to become leading authorities on politics and government. His two essays, which constitute the opening chapter in the book, are taken from one of his most important treatises with the permission of the MacMillan publishers. Appropriately, the first looks at the American presidency from the standpoint of changing perspectives and problems. The second may well be a minor classic on the neglected topic of the American style in politics.

Charles McDowell is the Washington correspondent of *The Richmond Times Dispatch* and a regular on the public affairs television program, Washington Week. In frequent columns and in a memorable address at the University of Virginia, McDowell calls for greater respect for politics and politicians. If politics is a dirty word in the American vocabulary, its importance to the survival of the American republic is also self-evident. McDowell appeals for a deeper understanding of the role politics plays.

I contribute an essay on "The President, Congress and Foreign Policy" drawing on a study of the subject by members of two influential groups, the Atlantic Council and the former Members of Congress. I served as rapporteur of the group and edited a volume of essays as well as writing the main policy paper. The present chapter is inspired by these various efforts.

Eugene V. Rostow is the former Dean of the Yale Law School. His brief essay on "The President as Commander in Chief" helps us understand another important dimension of presidential leadership.

Vietnam as an event in American foreign policy has left its imprint on every aspect of future policy and leadership. I have sought to explore some of the changes by looking at "Moral Contradictions or Political Consensus Before and After Vietnam."

A brillant young Harvard political scientist, Yuen Foong Khong, takes aim at the concept that American action in Korea provided an analogy for foreign policy in Vietnam. He asks whether another analogy may be the British effort in Malaya and the linkage of such analogies. The larger issue is what role do analogies play in highly variable historical situations.

Related to the question of analogies is the importance of persistent patterns in international politics. Are there certain recurrent forces in international politics that influence actions across time and place? Are these patterns associated with power, ethics, and statesmanship? Dr. Nicolai Petro and I look at these questions seeking to balance what is recurrent and unique in world politics. In the light of such circumstances, what then are the requirements of statesmanship for the future?

All issues of leadership are influenced in the last fifth of the twentieth century by the nuclear question. It has been said that the atomic bomb changed everything in international politics except our way of thinking. Professor Robert A. Strong of Tulane University explores the effects on political language of the demands for missile defense. In the future, nuclear war requirements are destined to effect longer issues of diplomacy and defense insofar as leadership is concerned.

The volume concludes with several essays on the future of leadership in which policies and past leaders are called on to advance understanding of these crucial issues. Don Mitchell, a staff aide to Senator John Glenn, has written an analysis of Adlai Stevenson as a model for leadership in the future. William H. Boley, a young theologian, contributes a paper on theological and ethical reflection addressed to Christian realism and liberation theology.

PART ONE

The President, Politics and Foreign Policy

The President

by
Herbert G. Nicholas

Viewed either in its dignified or in its efficient capacity, the Presidency
is the supreme unifying element in the American system of government.
The Supreme Court may symbolize and dispense the justice under law
without which the Union could not long survive. Congress may provide
voice and sinew for the multiple elements that make up the national mixture. But it is the President who speaks and acts for the nation as whole,
who takes at his inauguration the prescribed oath to 'preserve, protect and
defend the Constitution of the United States', and to whom the nation
looks, when all else fails, to take the decisions needed to preserve the
Union against internal disintegration or external threat. Fathers do not
bring up their children to be members of Congress, nor do many nourish
the hope of seeing their offspring on the Supreme Court, but there have
been few log cabins that, in popular imagination at least, did not
command an avenue which terminated in the White House.

To have been born of American parents, to have been fourteen years a
resident of the U.S.A., and thirty five years of age — these modest constitutional qualifications leave the career open to almost all talents, and
even the extra-constitutional requirements do not close it to many. Since
1960 it has not been necessary to be a Protestant, though it would be a
rash candidate who professed no Christian faith at all. It is still essential to
be either a Democrat or a Republican. (Of those candidates in recent
times who were not, LaFollette in 1924 came closest to success, and that
was not very close.) It is, apparently, helpful to be or have been a lawyer;
two-thirds of Presidents have been, while over half have had military
experience. Two-thirds have served in one house or other of Congress,
and a surprising number (thirteen) have been Vice-Presidents. But con-
sidering the nature of the Chief executive's office it is surprising that
fewer than a third have had previous experience of federal office-holding
and only fifteen have been state governors.

However, the qualifications, formal and informal, for the Presidency

3

do not give much clue to the essential nature of the job. This is *the* great American institution, its creation arguably the greatest achievement of the American political genius (what other country has been able to operate an elective monarchy for over 200 years without interruption?), the quadrennial contest for it *the* drama of American politics, the enjoyment of it perhaps the most exacting, as it is certainly the most lonely, task that any democratically elected official in the world can undertake. The spotlight of publicity never leaves the incumbent, or his family; successive Presidents, by seeking to cash in on an insatiable public curiosity about every detail of their private lives, from their golf handicap to their digestive processes, have left an ever smaller area of activity the incumbent can call his own. The White House combines the glamour of a palace, albeit a small one, with the intimacy of a home, and it is precisely that blend of the official and the personal which gives the Presidency its peculiar potency. As Bagehot said of Queen Victoria's monarchy, 'it brings down the pride of sovereignty to the level of petty life' and 'sweetens politics by the seasonable addition of nice and pretty events'. Possibly the domestic round at the White House is not quite as pretty (or at any rate as glamorous) as at Windsor, but in an age more sophisticated than Victoria's the American President may gain even more from the combination of being both a family man and a (four-year) prince. He is after all both monarch and prime minister, both head of state and head of government — a partisan government (he has won election on a party label) and yet a government of all the people.

This imposes strains. The dignified aspects of the office may call for attributes which the politician may lack. Not all of Lyndon Johnson's personal foibles were as well suited to the state rooms of the White House as to the *couloirs* of the Senate. A reforming President may arouse resentments, warranted or not, which may stand in his way when he has to speak to or for the whole nation; Woodrow Wilson and Franklin Roosevelt were victims of that. Every Presidency offers examples of failures to bring into identical focus the two images of the office. On the whole, however, what is remarkable about the American experience is the success that the United States has achieved in establishing and maintaining the democratic ideal of an elected monarch. Not every President succeeds in effecting the perfect combination of popular appeal and supra-party stature of a Lincoln, though Harry Truman in our time has demonstrated how this is still within the reach of a man of superficially ordinary talent. But time and time again at moments of crisis Presidents have been able to draw upon the inherited resources of their office to evoke from the country a response which transcends anything that mere party or personality could elicit. If the dual character of the office carries certain hazards it also confers certain unique advantages.

There is no royal road to the Presidency. The office is filled every four years by the man who is successful first in winning his party's nomination and then in carrying the ensuing election. In one sense this is a truly winnowing process. The contest is long and intense — never less than from winter to autumn — and involves contests in presidential primaries spread over five months or more, reaches its first peak in the nominating convention in July and August, and culminates in an all-out offensive from September to November. An athlete's stamina, a chameleon's adaptability, a lavish war chest, a loyal but not overly exclusive campaign team, a capacity both to elicit and to transcend party loyalty — these are the desirable attributes of a successful candidate. They are not, unfortunately, enough to guarantee success in office, as Presidents from Harding to Carter have discovered. For life in the White House there are other, increasingly essential, qualifications, in particular experience of executive office, which can actually be a handicap in the campaign (because executives have to disappoint as well as please), knowledge of the Washington establishment (once upon a time each President made his own, like Andrew Jackson; now he has to cope with a permanent nexus of office and influence), and finally and perhaps most indispensably, knowledge of and feeling for the international world beyond America's borders.

Obviously the paragon has not yet been made who is at all points equal to the challenges of the Presidency (and who can also get himself elected). In his absence there has been a strong temptation to fall back on the arts of opinion-manipulation for which their practitioners (and their critics) claim so much. Candidates can be packaged, Presidents can be sold, underdogs can become top dogs if the right strategies are adopted — this is the 'nothing is impossible' world of political advertising and public relations. It is permissible to doubt how much these artful practitioners can in fact deliver (cf. Ronald Reagan's low poll even in his so-called landslide victory of 1984), though of course it has to be admitted that where the margin of victory is small enough (0.2 per cent in 1960 for Kennedy) any factor can be adjudged crucial. The measuring rod which can assess such aids to victory has yet to be invented. But it is permissible to ask why so much dependence, at such expense, has come to be placed upon such meretricious and dubious mechanisms.

Part of the answer lies undoubtedly in the mesmeric effect of television, especially commercial television, since 1948. The seeming success of the new medium in selling sentiment, thrills, and detergents to the viewer encouraged the conviction that it could be similarly employed to sell him a President. Despite the gigantic deployment of talent and funds in the service of this operation it is by no means certain that the medium has produced the results attributed to it.[1] It is hard to think of candidates less 'telegenic' than Lyndon Johnson or Nixon or more photographically appealing than John Lindsay, yet the screen did not thwart the designs of the first two or rescue the fortunes of the third. What it has done, indubitably, is to heighten the hazards, the burdens, the superficiality and the costs of campaigning; the hazards because a gaffe on TV is a gaffe registered by millions; the burdens because TV has been superimposed on the existing chores of campaigning; the superficiality because the image, prepackaged, can easily override the argument, however cogent; the costs because television time is prodigiously expensive.

But behind the obvious appeal of TV as the all-purpose, wonder-working gimmick lies a more fundamental change in the nature of presidential candidacies. As recently as Franklin D. Roosevent a candidate won his nomination and conducted his campaign primarily through the mechanism as well as in the name of his party. Since 1952 he has been, by comparison, a lonely runner. Eisenhower did not win the nomination or the election as a Republican Party leader. He could have had the nomination of either party; he won on a broad wave of support that derived from his personal and wartime popularity. Eight years later John F. Kennedy returned the White House to the Democrats, but not by working through the 'regular' party organization. Instead he assembled his own team and financed it very largely by his own fortune. In the campaign, as in the White House, he kept his 'New Frontiersmen' distinct from the old party hacks. Lyndon Johnson, apprenticed as a New Dealer and deeply dyed in the party politics of House and Senate, nevertheless, when he campaigned for himself in 1964, built his own organization, on his Kennedy inheritance, rather than on the party in the country. Nixon, more than any of his predecessors, ran his own campaign with his own loyalists, from their own headquarters in New York City, in 1968 and 1972. At the opposite extreme George McGovern, Nixon's 1972 opponent, created his 'children's crusade' of ruthless idealists who were as much at odds with the conventional Democratic Party as with the Republicans. Carter's image in 1976 was in many ways a more conservative one, but he no less created his own team, basically Georgian, to win the nomination and, in office, to run the government; there were few debts outstanding when victory was won, either by White House to Congress or vice versa. Reagan in 1980 built his campaign around a team of carefully selected advisers, some from his base in California politics, some of them veterans of the Nixon presidential years. With these he conducted a highly personal offensive in virtually every presidential primary and by his sequence of successes arrived at the convention with the nomination assured.

As these examples suggest, in such a situation it does no harm to the presidential candidate for him to have generous campaign resources of his own. If he will not need them after nomination (and they may well be a help even then), he will certainly need them in the primaries. The public will not hold it against him, and his entourage will sleep better and work harder if they know that, come success or failure, his cheques will not bounce. That does not mean that the Presidency can be bought. As the fate of Nelson Rockefeller, who never quite made it to the altar, reminds us, it takes more than a dowry to make a bride. But what money can do for a candidate is to emancipate him from hand-to-mouth improvisations and dependencies, enable him to plan strategically rather than tactically, help him to negotiate with 'the interests' for a position of governmental independence.

Meanwhile, and irrespective of the personal independence of individual candidates, the weak, and incoherent American party has resulted in the development of a more detached, indeed isolated, Presidency, whose burdens have grown greater while its base has grown smaller. In such a situation, the President's Cabinet is of little help; British observers should not be deceived by the similarity of name into thinking that this is any kind of equivalent to Bagehot's 'hyphen which joins', and 'a buckle which fastens'. Far better to think of it as Professor Richard Fenno,[2] its most authoritative modern analyst, describes it, as 'the lengthened shadow of the Presidency'. It is indeed 'the President's Cabinet'. As such it is, very properly, not known to the Constitution. Nor are the extra-constitutional guidelines very clear or rigid. Its official membership is that of the heads of the established executive departments, those that have Secretaries, from State to Agriculture. But if membership is defined in terms of actual attendance, Cabinet membership is a much more fluid matter. Other agency heads will be called in as often and for as long as required. The Attorney General and the Director of the Office of Management and Budget (OMB) are likely to be regulars and it is a rare meeting that will not be attended by one or more members of the President's own White House staff. The result is a rather unreal collectivity, a body which can very rarely develop independent powers of deliberation, still less a will or policy of its own. And this for a very good reason — its members are there, ultimately, because the President has selected them to carry out his policies, not because they represent elements in his party or even sections of his constituents. Indeed, although at the inception of a new administration a President may take care, in making his principal appointments, that considerations of representativeness have due weight — that Catholics, Jews, Negroes, Southwesterners, women, trade unionists, right-wingers, left-wingers, etc. all have their place, two other considerations will inescapably dominate his subsequent replacement — loyalty and competence. Only the strongest of Presidents like Lincoln can tolerate rivals within their administration; only the most indulgent, like Franklin Roosevelt, can put up with executives who fall down on the job. Thus most Cabinets will consist not of broad-based, interchangeable, debate-minded all-rounders (the theory at least underlying British Cabinet membership) but of two recognizable types: those members who are experts in their own field — foreign affairs, say, or budget management — and those who represent a certain constituency — labour, agriculture, etc. — which the President cannot afford to ignore. The first group are unlikely to venture far outside their own specialities, the second are generally indifferent to considerations which do not have an immediate impact upon their constituents.

All this reduces the value of the Cabinet either as a sounding board which the President can use or as a forum in which a critic can bring to the President's notice any of those topics that monarchs, elected or unelected, prefer not to hear about. Memoirs of Cabinet members are replete with evidence of the barrenness of their collective deliberations and the assiduity with which each tries to catch the President's private ear after the plenary session is over. *Per contra* the open voicing of disagreements between Cabinet members which by British standards is a relatively frequent feature of American government, will have proportionately less serious consequences. Of course it is always better if members of an administration present a solid front to the world, but where it is recognized that Cabinet members have little responsibility for extra-departmental policy and do have an inescapable obligation to serve their constituents, in Congress or the country, the damage, if not the brouhaha, that ensues from these open breaches of unanimity can generally be sustained.

The unserviceability of the Cabinet as an instrument either of deliberation or co-ordination has led to an increased reliance on other devices. It was in the area of foreign and defence policy that the Cabinet's inadequacies — its diffuseness, its loose-lipped indifference to consistency or security — first necessitated the creation of another organ to advise the President and co-ordinate what the main departments were doing. This was the National Security Council, set up in 1947 in the wake of the U.S.A.'s wartime experience and also in emulation of what Americans had observed, as members of the wartime alliance, of the Defense

Committee of the British Cabinet. The N.S.C. consists essentially of the President, the Vice-President (a recognition in push-button warfare days of the need to try and guarantee continuity of command in the event of presidential incapacity), and the Secretaries of State and Defense; not the least of its strengths derives from its being serviced by a small and highly competent permanent staff directed by the President's assistant for National Security Affairs. The N.S.C. has introduced order, reflection, and planning into areas where decisions were previously taken too readily by hunch or departmental muscle. Even so, it would be a great mistake to regard it as an institution with any strength in its own right. When Nixon decided in December 1972 to try and end the Vietnam war by unleashing the whirlwind bombardment of North Vietnam he did not consult the N.S.C.; indeed the N.S.C. had not met in more than six months. It is essentially a presidential convenience, a device to be used, or ignored, as presidential taste or prudence may dictate.

Even more is this true of such experiments as have been made with a counterpart, the so-called Domestic Council, such as Nixon created in 1970, or the five Cabinet Councils set up by Reagan in 1981. They too had staff and the equivalent of a secretary. But they were conduits for decision-making as often by-passed as used, irregular in function, uncertain as to power. The truth is that every President likes to think he is running a freshly-minted model of orderly administration and each one blots the beauty of his organisational charts under the stresses of actual decision-making.

The President, all the same, is only one man. He must have assistance. In 1861 Abraham Lincoln had embarked on a Presidency and a civil war with only two secretaries and young ex-newspaperman to sort the mail. By 1933 Franklin Roosevelt had become aware that he would need something more than this if the United States government was going to cope with the Depression, and in 1939 he stabilized his expanded establishment in the form of the Executive Office of the President, in effect a White House secretariat that would enable him to exercise some measure of effective control over the sprawling ganglion which constitutes the federal government. Although repeatedly modified (generally in the direction of expansion) since Roosevelt's time, the structure still stands on his foundations. At its centre is the White House Office which serves the President directly and personally through his principal assistants or advisers, who will always include a press secretary, a presidential counsel, an appointments secretary, a congressional liaison officer, a speech writer, and an adviser on national security who will also be secretary to the N.S.C. Most Presidents have needed in addition an *alter ego*, lynchpin to this wheel, who could be their completely trusted confidant and right arm — Woodrow Wilson's Colonel House, Roosevelt's Harry Hopkins, Eisenhower's Sherman Adams, Kennedy's Theodore Sorensen, Nixon's Bob Haldeman, Carter's Hamilton Jordan, Reagan's James Baker — but each had his own method of organizing the office as a whole, from Roosevelt's 'creative chaos' to Eisenhower's army-style channels of command. Presidents have similarly differed as to the range of functions which they have wished to keep under their personal control, though most modern administrations have agreed that foreign policy is an area which the White House can never leave to the formally responsible department, State. In consequence the President's foreign policy assistant, be he a Bundy, a Kissinger, or a Brzezinski, is always more than a liaison officer, or even a watchdog to see that the President's policies are properly executed. He is, at the very least, something very close to being a second Secretary of State; sometimes like Kissinger he is the *de facto* Secretary whatever his location.

The expansion, in size and complexity, of the Executive Office of the President has led to a good deal of loose talk about the Presidency having become 'institutionalized'. This idea enjoyed particular currency during Eisenhower's presidential incapacities when the impression was deftly conveyed by James Hagerty, his press officer, that the work of the office could be conducted in the chief's absence through the machinery of Cabinet and aides. In reality this fiction was sustained only by some dubiously constitutional exercise of power on the part of Sherman Adams, and the President's remarkable powers of recuperation. The truth is that the Presidency is far too personal an office ever to be truly institutionalized,[3] and indeed, by Whitehall standards, the White House Office is even less institutionalized than No. 10. There is almost total fluidity in the top appointments, which change with each President, and hardly less flexibility in the shape and organization of the whole — in each case for the same reason, a new President's need to run things his own way.

The most nearly institutionalized part of the Presidency is something which in Whitehall would be housed in the Treasury. From 1921 to 1929 a Bureau of the Budget was indeed housed in the U.S. Treasury, but as part of the White House reforms of that year it was brought directly under presidential control, with the responsibility not merely of preparing annual budgets but also of using the power of the purse to keep the executive departments under tighter control. Reorganized and renamed in 1970 as the Office of Management and Budget (O.M.B.), the office is the drafting agency for the President's executive orders and proclamations and, even more important, is the clearing-house through which each department's proposals for new legislation must pass before they can be presented to Congress for its consideration. If there is a single, all-purpose institution of administrative control in Washington, this is it.

The figure at the apex of this pyramid, the human official in whose service and likeness this apparatus is constructed, is pre-eminently a man of power. This is something that follows from the size and might of the United States and from his position as the country's chief executive. But because his is a *constitutional* power we still have to ask exactly what it amounts to. Discrepant answers echo back to us from previous holders of the office. 'The President is at liberty, both in law and conscience,' wrote Woodrow Wilson, 'to be as big a man as he can. His capacity will set the limit.' 'I sit here all day', said Harry Truman, 'trying to persuade people to do the things they ought to have sense enough to do without my persuading them. That's all the powers of the President amount to.' The Presidency, of course, has not stood still, either from Wilson's time to Truman's, or since. But its movement, until the excesses of Watergate were exposed, was almost wholly in one direction — towards self-aggrandizement. If Wilson sounded expansionary and Truman frustrated, it is because the one wrote when the pressures on the office and the aspirations of its holder were still comparatively modest, and the second registered his ironic protest when squeezed between constitutionalist critics and impatient clients. They reflect the contrast between an America with a modestly reforming government on a virtually island continent and an America whose daily bread and hourly security are inescapably dependent on decisions taken in the White House, often in response to happenings a hemisphere away.

In domestic politics this has led to an expectation of and a dependence on presidential leadership which seems irreversible. There is no evidence that in face of the vastly greater demands made on modern government Congress can itself provide a substitute for presidential leadership. The United States will never see in the White House another Ulyssess S. Grant, with his conviction that the Presidency was 'a purely administrative officer'. Indeed the Constitution itself forbids as much. Why else the provisions for presidential messages and presidential vetoes? Even Ford in his posture of presidential modesty after Watergate reached out for the veto on 66 occasions in two years and had fewer than 1 in 5 of them overruled. The constitutional battle is therefore joined on a comparatively limited front.

A limited front, but within its limits a confused and uncertain one. Thus the so-called legislative veto has been utilized by Congress since 1932, but has vastly increased, in frequency and significance, with the rise in Congressional assertiveness which the 'imperial presidencies' of Johnson and Nixon provoked. The legislative veto is a statutory provision that allows one or both houses of Congress to disapprove or hold in abeyance an action of the executive branch. At first sight it seems a clear shifting of the constitutional frontier in favour of Congress. The legislative veto has nevertheless survived presidential protests and has not yet been found unconstitutional by the Supreme Court. The reason is not far to seek. The restrictions that the veto imposes are the reverse side of the coin to the powers that Congress delegates. This was well illustrated by the history of impoundment. Nixon's refusal to spend money that Congress had voted for programmes of which he disapproved provoked the legislature into passing the 1974 Impoundment Control Act. But this did not prohibit impoundment as such; instead it recognised the power of the President to defer the spending of appropriated funds, but made such deferral subject to a Congressional resolution. In other words it recognised that the boundaries of presidential and congressional power had to be re-drawn. It did not seek a total acquisition of territory for either side, and in fact left it for future usage to decide whether the effect was to curb the President's independence or to concede some of the legislature's dearly cherished control of the purse.

The truth is that such intricate and ragged disputes are unlikely to yield to neat or merely legal solutions. What is ultimately at issue is the power of the President, working through public opinion, to get Congress to see things his way, with his formal constitutional and legal instruments mere ancillaries to his basic ability — or lack of it — to move the nation and its elected representatives by persuasion. Whether, beyond that, he has some kind of extra-constitutional residue of power to 'save' the nation, in the event of a congressional failure to act, is a somewhat scholastic question, much agitated at the time of the New Deal and always capable of being resuscitated in moments of crisis, but belonging ultimately to the realm of abstraction rather than practical politics. If crisis demands action and the right President is there to take it, he will act, and Congress and the courts will ratify his course afterwards (or disallow it after it has ceased to matter, like the disallowance of the N.R.A. in 1935). If the crisis does not warrant it or the wrong President is in charge, he will be impeached. The problem here is ultimately not a constitutional but a political one — whether a President can establish and maintain, either by personal authority or through his leadership of his party, a response from Congress which will sustain him not just at one moment or another but throughout the years which are needed to promulgate and carry through a policy.

In the area of foreign (and in this I include defense) policy the factors at work are different. In the first place the decline of party, so complicating and, as it were, debilitating, in domestic policy, does not have comparable consequences here. Party has seldom been a clear or clarifying factor in American foreign policy debates and its weakening has done little to diminish the President's potentialities in this sphere. Secondly, whereas the nineteenth-century President was more likely to meet a crisis on the domestic than on the foreign front, in the twentieth century the exact reverse is true. The domestic norm is still that of a predictable course of events at which both President and Congress can make reasonable guesses and for which both are equipped by previous experience. Where foreign affairs are concerned there is no norm; there is a permanent latent crisis. This grimly symbolized by the 'black box' which accompanies a modern President wherever he goes and which contains the cryptograms he would employ if he had to press the nuclear button. There is no black box, there are no cryptograms, there is no nuclear button where domestic policies are concerned.

The power of the President in foreign affairs has received such striking demonstration in the era of the Cold War that it has seemed to some observers that there are, in effect, two Presidencies. Presidents who have been thwarted or defeated by Congress on their domestic programmes have succeeded time and time again in persuading Congress to acquiesce in their foreign policies. It was on its triumphs — or its excesses — in foreign policy that the 'Imperial Presidency' of the 1960s and '70s was built. This concept of the President as a solo virtuoso was almost certainly not shared by the Founding Fathers who envisaged the constitutional provision about seeking the 'advise and consent' of the Senate as committing the President to utilizing that chamber as a kind of council of state where foreign affairs were concerned. The Senators were after all to be the authorized spokesmen for the constitutent parts of the Union. When there were only thirteen states and twenty six Senators, and when foreign policy-making lacked day-to-day urgency, such a system might have worked — though, significantly perhaps, it was not seriously tried even at the outset. But as the federation grew and Senators multiplied, consultation shrank to the bare level required to meet the inescapable constitutional requirement that the President 'make Treaties, provided two-thirds of the Senators present concur' (Article II, Section ii, §2). Even so, as long as foreign policy revolved around the treaty-making process, the Senate Cerberus was a monster that every President had to respect and mollify. Even in the twentieth century, down to the time of Truman, the President had to measure his actions in foreign policy by the pace of the Senate — this despite the fact that by now foreign policy had acquired an urgency and priority unconceived of in 1789.

What emancipated the Presidency? It is hard to doubt that it was the invention of the atom bomb. Its potentialities for swift and total destruction, the problems of devising a safe and secret procedure of control, its early acquisition by a rival sovereign state — all this put into the President's hands a power which, whether he wanted to or not, he could not lodge elsewhere. It increased his stature and exclusiveness overnight. And although this was a weapon of war, its deadly 'brightness of a thousand suns' irradiated the President's peacetime diplomacy as well. Foreign policy-making henceforth was inevitably conducted in a new awareness of how swiftly irreversible a faulty step could be. The diplomacy of the Cuban missile crisis was not something which could be accommodated to traditional constitutional processes.

It is open to debate whether it was by historical coincidence or by the logic of its own implications, but, whichever it was, the atom bomb was evolved and, so to say, administered in the context of alliance diplomacy. The President who thus acquired an absolute weapon also involved his country in a set of permanent alliance commitments that had no parallel in American history. And just as only the President could control the bomb, so only the President could effectively run NATO and the U.S.A.'s other diplomatic-military arrangements whenever comparable elements of urgency and secrecy were involved.

The constitutional underpinnings of this new, exalted, and emancipated Presidency were already available once the lawyers and historians started to look for them. Perhaps the most adaptable and convenient formula was the one inherent in the deceptively simple label which the Constitution conferred on the President in making him 'Commander-in-Chief' of the Army, Navy, and militia (Article II, Section ii, §1). Out of this Lincoln had conjured the power to impose a blockade, raise a volunteer army, expand the regular army and navy, suspend *habeas corpus*, introduce conscription, and issue the Emancipation Proclamation — all without congressional authorization.

Second only to this was the undermining of the Senate's exclusive control over treaty-making. The instrument to hand for this purpose was the President's claimed right to negotiate 'executive agreements' with foreign powers. This had a long and respectable lineage, from the Rush-Bagot agreement of 1817 establishing disarmament in the Great Lakes to the Lansing-Ishii agreement of 1917 which recognized Japan's 'special rights' in China. But it was World War II and its aftermath that really brought the executive agreement into its own, as the points of contact and potential friction between the U.S.A. and other powers multiplied, and so necessitated a faster and more flexible range of negotiating instruments than the treaty-making process could provide. The numbers negotiated have now run into thousands, the ratio of executive agreements to treaties has risen from 1.5:1 to 15:1, and the courts have fully upheld their validity and enforceability in law. It is by such agreements that the U.S.A. maintains many of its bases overseas, provides much of its military assistance to its allies, and indeed operates a major part of its alliance diplomacy. This does not mean, of course, that anything that required a treaty can now be accomplished by executive agreement. There persists a consensus about what is 'expected' by Senate and foreign negotiators alike, a consensus determined partly by precedent, partly by prestige. The future of the Panama Canal, like its original conception, is still felt to need a senatorial blessing. But the range of topics for which a presidential laying on of hands suffices has grown longer every year.

In these twilight zones of modern diplomacy it was not to be expected that the other congressional prerogative (shared between House and Senate), the right to declare war, could retain much vitality. Hardly was the ink dry on this clause of the Constitution (Article I, Section viii, §11) than the illusoriness of its claims became apparent. In order to occur war does not have to be 'declared'. It can come, as the universe came to Margaret Fuller, and simply insist on being accepted. In only one instance, the War of 1812, did Congress use its full-blooded power to make a declaration of war. In 1846 with Mexico, in 1898 with Spain, in 1917 and 1941 in the two World Wars, Congress simply recognized that a war did in fact exist. In addition there have been over 150 occasions (161 were listed by the Library of Congress in 1970) on which the United States has used armed force abroad without any congressional declaration of war, mainly under the President's authority (and obligation) to protect American life, property, and vital interests. Truman in 1950 involved the United States in a conflict in Korea (justified as a 'police action' under the auspices of the United Nations), which cost 33,000 American lives and nearly 160,000 American casualties, without any formal authorization by Congress at all. The long, steady, deepening involvement in Vietnam began as presidential 'defensive' action, followed by the Tonkin Gulf resolution of 1964, a congressional resolution which by-passed the issue of a declaration of war by authorizing the President 'to take all necessary measures....to prevent further aggression' and setting the whole affair in a context of response to an attack on U.S. naval vessels. From this developed an all-out but still undeclared war fought 'defensively' and extended, under the doctrine of 'hot pursuit', into Thailand, Laos, and Cambodia.

It was the hubristic excesses (and disasters) of the Vietnam war which impelled the nation to look afresh at the President's sweeping powers in foreign policy and war-making. The result was the passage of the War Powers Resolution in 1973 which obliged the President to report to Congress within forty-eight hours of committing armed forces abroad. The use of such forces would have to end within sixty days unless Congress authorized a longer period. A further thirty days' grace was permitted to ensure 'safe withdrawal'. What exactly is the Resolution's effect? Does it prevent future Vietnams? Johnson, after all, had 'reported', however deceptively, to Congress in 1964 and 1965 and Congress had certainly given him an endorsement which, as he said, was like 'Grandma's nightdress': 'it covered everything.' Did the War Powers Resolution perhaps even enhance the President's power by authorizing 'sixty-day wars'?

Time alone can provide reliable answers to such questions, but the mere fact that they can be asked demonstrates once again the peculiarly exposed and ambiguous position of the Presidency. Expected, in a crisis, to do whatever is necessary, the President yet lacks for day-to-day purposes of government the kind of politico-constitutional radar that a parliamentary system can provide a responsive executive. He cannot get an advisory opinion from the courts; they will pronounce only after the deed. He cannot get a disinterested ruling from his Congress, and even to seek it is to run the risk of making a damaging admission of infirmity of purpose. He cannot get it from his party, since it no longer exists in a serious institutional form. He cannot get it from his Cabinet because it is a nonentity. He can only get it from his entourage in those very rare cases where there is a courtier honest and bold enough to tell the truth, however unpalatable; there are not many Roosevelts fortunate enough to have a Harry Hopkins. There remains only one sounding board disinterested and yet informed, politically sagacious but not committed to any single political cause. This is the press or, to be more comprehensive, the media.

The chart of relationships between American Presidents and the media is a long and fluctuating one, but, with allowances made for temporary divagations, it moves in only one direction, towards a greater, if not necessarily a more compatible, intimacy. In this as in so many other areas the Roosevelt era seems to be a watershed. The New Deal's impact on everybody, the new type of leadership that Roosevelt provided, the inadequacies of Congress and congressional Democrats in particular as intermediaries in this process — all combined to direct Roosevelt's attention to the potentialities for influence that the media offered, particularly the new medium of broadcasting. For the first time a President could appeal to the electorate personally, in their own homes, by the device of the 'fireside chat', informal, unforceful, but oh how insidious! All intermediaries, constitutional or institutional, were bypassed. The people's leader spoke directly to his flock. Moreover, by the regularity and intimacy of his weekly press conferences and the network of White

House-press liaisons that his aides maintained, Roosevelt was able to use the press as his eyes and ears, antennae that could reach beyond White House and Capitol Hill to tell him what the readers of that press were thinking.

Since Roosevelt there has been progress, if that is the word, in only one direction. No President, with the marginal exception of Kennedy, has had an equally deft and delicate relationship with the press corps, combining ability to play on that extremely fine-tuned instrument with an ear sensitive enough to catch accurately the echoes that rebound from it. The temptation, always latent, which indeed Roosevelt himself did not always resist, is to treat the press merely as something to be manipulated. The coming of television has intensified this.

The ability to put one's image, 'in living colour', even if so far in only two dimensions, into the voter's living room has acted on Presidents like a wonder drug on athletes. They fear its consequences but cannot resist its potentialities. The superficialities of appearance count far more than ever; the message is in permanent risk of being subordinated to the medium. In a country where virtually all television is commercial it brings with it to a degree that even the most crassly commercial of newspapers never did the values of the market-place. The calculations of politics become the higher mathematics of market research. The fact that nothing can be conclusively proved about the reliability of such research has not prevented its gurus acquiring an ascendancy in the planning of campaigns and the presentation of policies which far exceeds the grubby influences exerted on the White House by the potential bosses of yore. Moreover the intrinsic costliness of the medium has, as we have seen, added enormously to the expense of campaigning, with far-reaching implications for the democratic ideal of making the processes of politics open to all.

Worst of all, though, is the intrinsically one-way nature of the medium. A Roosevelt 'manipulating' the press is still a human being talking to and, at least in some measure, obliged to listen to a *corps d'élite* of political observers who do more than reproduce their master's voice. They analyse it, comment on it, criticize it. It is going too far, as some enthusiasts have done, to equate the presidential press conference, even in its heyday, with Question Time in the House of Commons. Even the boldest of journalists is not an adequate sparring partner for the elected tribune of the sovereign people, and where the President is one and the press corps are many most of the advantages of manoeuvre lie with him. But with appropriate allowances made, the Washington press corps, which for knowledgeability and assiduity has no equal in the world, does fill a gap which as we have seen threatens seriously to impair the healthy functioning of the Presidency. Both collectively and sometimes individually, as in the instances of influential journals like the *New York Times* and the *Washington Post*, the press is a power in its own right, something which a President can no more ignore than the rival organs of government. It constitutes, without doubt, an establishment, and, like all establishments, it has its tastes and its biases. It has obvious other weaknesses, the commercialism and pomposity of some of its proprietors, and the vanity and pretentiousness of some of its prima donnas; but, despite increasing concentrations of ownership, it still reflects the genuine diversity of America, and despite the tireless seductions of those who seek its favours it still preserves a high professional integrity. What it would mean to American institutions, and especially to the modern Presidency, if these qualities were lost, can readily be imagined if one tries to envisage Watergate without the exposures that blew it skyhigh.

Unfortunately television, not because of any lack of integrity or courage by individual reporters or teams, but by the essential nature of the medium, is incapable of doing an analogous job, while the temptations which it offers to a President without scruples are only too obvious. It was no accident that Nixon in 1972 campaigned almost entirely on TV or that during his Presidencies he held far fewer press conferences than any other President of modern times. Obviously no President, and no democracy, is going to dispense with the facility that television affords of presenting the image of the ruler directly to the ruled. Nor should it be impossible to control and limit the advantages that this, left to itself, must confer on the incumbent as against his critics. What no regulations or controls can do is to protect the monarch from the image of himself, from the isolation of the man in the studio, from the illusion that because he speaks to millions and is seen by millions he is therefore truly representing them. In this sense television heightens the burdens on the President by insulating him still further from reality. It leaves him with his central problem, of communication, further from solution than ever, because that problem is not the problem of communicating to, but of receiving communications from the multiple groups and entities that make up the country he has to lead. Without a firm party base, without an easy or regular dialogue with the legislature, without near-equals in Cabinet, the President is more nearly insulated in the second half of the twentieth century than at any previous period in American history. How to overcome this, while still preserving the proper prerogatives of his office, is the central problem for the modern President.

The Style of American Politics

by
Herbert G. Nicholas

That there is in the United States a national style of politics admits of no doubt. What that style consists of is less easy to define. This is a large country and a diverse society whose constituent communities have their origins in widely different times and circumstances. These diversities leave their mark on the mode of doing political business even when that business is directed in the first instance, as we have seen it is, to the establishment of a national government. An artificial capital, such as Washington was, created almost from nothing to avoid any too-emphatic pre-existing local attachment; a consciously contrived constitution designed to emphasize national unity and contain aspiring diversities — these might have been expected to result in a national style which, like the street plan of the federal city itself, emphasized regularities, directness, and symmetry and reflected as little as possible of the local topographical diversities. Yet just as in the city of Washington neighbourhoods have emerged to assert their local and often incongruous character against L'Enfant's grand urban design, so certain distinctive and recognizable elements in American life have come to exercise powerfully formative influences upon the nation's political style.

The first and most obvious of these is the South. The South is only *a* region in the national whole, not the richest, nor the most populous, nor arguably in its own domestic characteristics the most typically 'American'. But, with the possible exception of New England, it is the most clearly defined region in the country, with the strongest and most nearly consolidated and best preserved conviction of its historic identity. Its role at all stages in the development of the national community was crucial, often dominant. Within the limits imposed by its own 'peculiar institution' of slavery, it embraced with more devotion and consistency than any other part of the country the doctrine which, as we have seen, is not naturally American, of the primacy of politics. It was into politics more than into any other profession that, from the earliest times, the South put its ablest talents.[4] It was only when the last political device had been exhausted that the South turned, disastrously, to dissension and to arms; defeated and forcibly reunited, it relied once again, and this time ever more successfully, upon its skills in politics to make up for its weaknesses on the battlefield, in the counting-house, and in the workshop.

In this the South was certainly aided by the Hamilton-Jefferson bargain of 1790 by which the federal capital was established, within ten years' time, on the banks of the Potomac. From 1800 onwards the South enjoyed indubitable benefits from having the District of Columbia on its borders — indeed virtually within them, since Maryland, on the District's northern side, was hardly less Southern in character than Virginia on the other side. What would have been the effects on the operation of American government had Philadelphia in the Middle Colonies remained what in the 1780s it seemed to be, the natural capital of the United States? Or what if the ten-year interlude at New York had been perpetuated? Would New England then have learnt to exert on the banks of the Hudson the pressures and persuasions that the South so adeptly employed on the banks of the Potomac?

What is the Southern contribution to the American political style? A certain conservatism, of course; that goes without saying in the region so long identified with a one-party system. But in style as apart from substance the dominant feature of Southern conservatism is its reliance on procedural devices and technicalities as instruments for resisting change in a situation where numbers are in themselves inadequate to do the job. Seizing upon the minority safeguards written (often at their instigation) into the Constitution, Southerners, more than any other of America's numerous minorities, carried them into every nook and cranny of federal institutions, particularly into the legislature. The most artistic as well as the most muscular wielders of the filibuster have been Southerners. But this characteristic Southern weapon, with its opportunities for colourful oratorical display as well as sheer 'lung-evity', is merely the most dramatic and uncomplicated of the procedural devices which have been developed time and time again by Southern legislators, to maximize minority influence and frustrate majority impatience. Slow and delayed voting procedures, manipulation of quorum requirements, holdups in committees — these and a host of other devices make the procedures of Congress as intricate and, to the inexpert, as cumbersome as those of any legislature in the world, and in the preservation and exploitation of such resources the Southerners have always been pre-eminent. In this nothing has served them so well as their manipulation of the so-called seniority principle. Under the guise of deference to age which, surprising though it may seem in a self-consciously 'young' country, is one of

America's most conspicuous characteristics, the South fastened on House and Senate a system by which the key positions of committee chairman were filled according to length of uninterrupted congressional service — in other words success in securing re-election. And since the South, with its one-party system, easily led the nation in safe seats, it was Southerners who time and time again, and out of all proportion to their numbers, filled the committee chairmanships and held, in consequence, the levers of legislative power.

'Old Southern Home' was what William S. White, experienced reporter of the Senate, entitled the chamber in which this Southern dominance was most pronounced. In the Senate, as White says, 'the acceptable definitions' of what is proper, there and elsewhere, are far more often made by Southerners...than by all the rest of the place put together'.[5]

What is proper in Southern eyes, in the Senate and elsewhere, is the first instance a style of political rhetoric largely extinct in Britain but still persisting in American politics despite the pressures of the advertiser and the TV camera. It is the rhetoric of the old South, but not confined to the South — a high-flying invocation of abstract sentiments and moralities, in which content, where not eliminable, must always take second place to sound and form. Emphatically Southern, but again not exclusively so, are the frequently biblical overtones of this oratory. Scripture is more often invoked in American politics than anywhere else in the western world; not only is the Senate still Protestant: the Protestantism is the Protestantism of the Good Book.

But if at one end this rhetoric is high-flying and scriptural, at the other it is relaxed and anecdotal. Debate is rare in American politics, at any level, but talk looms large, is indeed frequently of the essence. Here again the Southern influence is very evident. As Cleanth Brooks said in another connection, the natural art-form of the South is the story. Almost a century ago Bryce remarked on the popular fondness for anecdotes, 'sometimes pushed to excess'. The relaxed, sometimes rambling anecdote set ideally in some rural or small-town context, preferably in the speaker's own state or district, and bringing out the earthy wisdom or shrewdness of the hay-seed or rustic worthy, is an ornament of political oratory which does not come amiss in any section of the country but which is an almost obligatory part of the equipment of any aspiring Southern politician.

That this 'folksy', easy-paced, good-humoured style can coexist with vehemence and passion is well exemplified in the political oratory of figures such as the populist Tom Watson, and Huey Long. The South has always recognized that persuasiveness, good humour, a mastery of the parliamentary rule book, and even the protective provisions of the Constitution itself may in the last resort prove inadequate. It has thus, as an embattled minority, never hesitated to bring into American politics the language — and of course the actions — of total resistance. It is the American Ulster (no mere analogy either, when so much Scotch-Irish blood runs in Southern veins) which 'will fight' and find full justification in its own conviction that it 'will be right'. The fire-eater has been pre-eminently a Southern gift to American politics. William Yancey, Barnwell Rhett, John C. Calhoun before the Civil War, 'Pitchfork' Ben Tillman after it, and Strom Thurmond and George Wallace in own time — the list could bear almost indefinite extension — they have all brought into politics the bland assumption that when the peaceful and legal processes of democracy were exhausted it was right and inevitable that extra-legal and violent practices should take over. Thus, as W.J. Cash, that most unsparing critic of his own people, put it, they helped to develop in the South (and, he might have added, elsewhere) 'that most dangerous of philosophies: the philosophy that, if only the end be reckoned good, the most damnable means become justifiable and even glorious'.[6]

No other region has left so pronounced a stamp on American politics as the South, if only because, as we have seen, no other part of the United States has retained so pronounced a regional character. New England, powerful as it was in the early years of the republic, suffered for its very success in commerce, industry, westward expansion, and immigrant influx a dilution of its puritanical, Greek, 'town meeting', democratic dedication. Its most successful political export was perhaps significantly in local government — the 'township', the relatively compact settlement managing its own affairs by the equal voice of all its widely diffused property owners. The tight-fisted, high- (and narrowly) principled, legally scrupulous, matter-of-fact democracy of New England represents indeed a mode of doing political business which has left its mark all over America, especially in the Middle West and Northwest, and of course it has its reflection on the national scene whether in figures of caricature like Calvin Coolidge or in family dynasties like the Cabots and Saltonstalls.

But while defeat in the Civil War made politics vital to the South, victory in the contest left New England free to act on Coolidge's principle that the business of America is business, and so to leave a vacuum of political leadership which had to be otherwise filled. If, however, politics means the resolution of conflicts by methods short of war — a task in which, with the conspicuous exception of the years 1861-5, American

politics has been pretty successful — then obviously neither the South
nor New England was ideally suited to be the nation's mentor. The one-
party intransigence of the first and the hyper-moralistic style of the
second were ill-suited to breed the skills of adjustment and compromise
that such a role requires. Significantly it was from the border states that
the 'great compromiser' Henry Clay and the would-be 'binder-up' of 'the
nation's wounds', Abraham Lincoln, were drawn. But in fact it was not
from any region or overlap of regions that America learnt her most
polished skills of political adjustment; it was from the largest and most
vocal of her immigrant groups, 'immigrant' being here defined illogical-
ly as 'of non-English or Scottish stock'. This group is, of course, the
Irish.

The peculiar impact of the Irish on American politics derived from
their dual role as simultaneously outsiders and insiders. Outsiders not
only because, like any immigrant group, they were the new boys in the
established community, poor, ignorant, competing for the meanest jobs,
but also because, in a Protestant country, they were patently and tena-
ciously Catholic, and remained so even when success had eliminated
cruder differentials. They were insiders, however, in a way that
Germans, Italians, or Slavs were not; though proudly non-English, they
spoke the language of their conquerors — even if in their own colourful
vernacular — and their political tradition derived, even if only through
opposition and by victimization, from the same set of Anglo-Saxon laws
and institutions that had shaped the U.S.A's. They were familiar, in
short, with those processes of political association, of debate, of elections
which were still strange to their fellow immigrants from other (particularly other Catholic) lands. They were thus uniquely equipped to take their
place in American politics and to shape and adjust that politics to the
needs and purposes of other immigrant groups besides themselves.
Whereas English and Scottish immigrants inserted themselves as individuals unobtrusively into the interstices of the existing political
community, accepting its leadership, its codes, and its constraints, the
Irish retained their group identity and solidarity and utilized their ready
comprehension of the system to facilitate not their acceptance of it but the
shaping of it to meet their needs — pre-eminently their needs as a group
only too familiar with its potentialities for victimization. They were
determined not to reproduce in America what they had left Ireland to
escape.

The solidarity that was instinctive with the Irish translated itself into a
clannish network of family relationships which was ready-made for
political success. This indeed the South, intensely family-conscious, had
already discovered, and there is much in common between region and

group in this regard, not least the emphasis on loyalty and 'regularity' thus engendered, and the subordination of issues to personalities. But whereas the South used this to cement a single-party system, the Irish used it to strengthen their side in a two-party conflict.

The enlarged family, the gang or the clan, turned insensibly into the machine. Its starting point was that the function of politics is not democratic participation *per se* — the town meeting — nor yet the selection of the best men to rule — 'public office as a public trust' — but the establishment by 'our' side of a lien on the disposable assets of government: jobs, contracts, franchises, pardons. In a materialist society in which the levers of government were all too often in the hands of business or other oligarchies (generally WASP to boot), the Irish designed their urban (and in a few cases rural) machines partly to wrest power away from the establishment, or, more generally because more feasibly, to make the party itself a kind of alternative government: a dispenser of loaves and fishes, a multiplier of jobs, a complicator (and so an indispensable manipulator) of the electoral process, a welfare agency in a society which held economy in government to be the highest civic virtue.

'The Irish,' as William Shannon well puts it in *The American Irish*, the most numerous and advanced section of the immigrant community, took over the political party (usually the Democratic Party) at the local level and converted it into virtually a parallel system of government. The network of party clubhouses and the hierarchy of party committees with a citywide leader or 'boss' at the apex constituted a 'shadow government', a supplementary structure of power that performed some functions more vital than those of the nominal, legal government. The main objective of the party, of course, was to capture control of the city government, but even when the party was out of office, it could continue to function. It had revenue from the 'tax' it levied upon saloons, houses of prostitution, gamblers and contractors. Out of these funds, the party machine could provide the food and coal it gave to those who were destitute. It could finance the young lawyers who interceded in court for the delinquent, wrote letters home to the old country for the illiterate, and intervened at city hall for those bewildered by the regulations and intricacies of the government. It could pay for the torchlight parades, the children's picnics, and the one-day excursion trips up the river or to the beach which brought recreation and a touch of colour to the lives of working-class families.[7]

What the Irish learnt for themselves, they taught to those who came after — or, to be more precise, as successive immigrant groups emerged from tutelage, the Irish master-minded their induction into American political society. The Irish did not yield up their primacy to those who came later; instead they contrived to keep it by setting the terms on which newer groups could be cut in on the privileges and power that the machine conferred. They contrived the balanced ticket, providing due recognition for race, religion, and national origin, as and when these factors established their claims, on behalf of each group, for recognition. They thus promoted the peaceful assimilation of their fellow immigrants to the American system — a remarkable feat, seldom paralleled in other multi-racial societies — and at the same time preserved and stimulated an interest, their own and that of their clients, in maintaining ethnic identities, in emphasizing distinctiveness and exclusiveness and thus retarding the realization of the American goal of society as the open pyramid, openly climbed.

A politics of clan and family had, of course, a particular appeal in a country of space and mobility, where the great American loneliness, familiar alike to frontiersmen and to the newcomer in the faceless metropolis, was always demanding positive counter-action. all politics is an exercise in unification, in the bringing together of people, but American politics is conspicuous for its insistence on the symbols of fraternity and cohesion — its profligate employment of first names and engaging sobriquets, its obsession with localism and the small-town ethos, its kissing of babies and 'pressing of the flesh'. No doubt even without Irish stimulus politicians would have developed their own techniques for bridging the gaps that America's size and diversity impose; but a training in Irish ward politics was a powerful help, if only because the Irish style became, as it were, the universal style. Among politicians the rule soon established itself, 'When in doubt, be Irish.'

'Easygoing' is the obvious epithet for this style in politics, and while the machine did sometimes have its oppressive side, especially in links with the rackets of the underworld, it sought in the main to operate on a live-and-let-live basis. Occasionally it did seek to establish a total monopoly of power and privilege within its own territory, but although of course it sought to bend the rules in every way to its own advantage it generally recognized that there were certain rules, certain democratic forms — the party system, legislatures, elections, courts. Bosses die in bed. Huey Long was an exception, and if from his assassination it can validly be deduced that he was establishing in Louisiana a dictatorship which seemingly admitted of no peaceable termination, his is an exception which proves the rule. In more senses than one the Louisiana of

Long's heyday was a banana republic — 'I am the Democratic Party in Louisiana.' For all the gothic extravagances of some other Southern one-party states, none has installed and supported a comparably dictatorial populism. Frank J. ('I am the Law') Hague of Jersey City fully justified his sobriquet by a sustained and corrupt manipulation of legal and administrative machinery in Hudson County, New Jersey, but his excesses were necessarily local and his reach limited.

In essence what the boss did was to milk the system by every means in his power, but to remain within the system. 'If you can't beat 'em join 'em.' 'What is the law between friends?' The ethos incarnated in these and similar maxims reflects no doubt a very un-Platonic concept of guardianship, but it is at least arguable that it made possible the induction into the political system of a whole range of voters who would never have understood, still less operated, a more rigid, more law-respecting, and less personal form of public administration. Indeed at the other extreme too it had a function to perform. Behind the strict public morals of the New England Brahmins lay an oversimplified concept of the functions of the moral law in politics. The Supreme Court often does and often should follow the electoral returns, but this was truth more readily realized by Mr. Dooley than by the legal formalists who graced the bench. That politics is first and foremost a way of enabling men to live together — insistence on this was the supreme gift of the politician to the American polity.

In 1943 the Democratic Senator from Indiana, Frederick Van Nuys, saluted his old Republican rival, Jim Watson, on his retirement from politics. He asked what characteristics had made Jim Watson successful, and went on to provide his own answers:

> First, he is one of the best story-tellers in America....Second, Jim Watson is a shrewd observer and a keen politician....To my certain knowledge he at one time belonged to 28 different fraternal orders and scores of similar organizations. In 'jineing' up Jim never let a little thing like consistency interfere with his activities.
>
> For instance, at one and the same time he was affiliated with the Ancient Order of Hibernians and *sub rosa*, of course, the directing head of the Ku Klux Klan. For years he carried an honorary membership in the bartenders' union, and during the same time was the most vociferous advocate and defender of the Women's Christian Temperance Union. During prohibition, he outrivaled Carrie Nation on the stump but knew the back door of every drug store in Indiana. (*Laughter.*)

Yes, Jim was a great campaigner. He has kissed more babies, coddled more mothers, eaten more cold mashed potatoes and head lettuce with Thousand Island dressing at political banquets, listened to more long-winded introductory speeches, slept in more cold spare bedrooms, promised more jobs, and slapped more people on the back than any other ten men in the United States of America.

To boil it all down, Jim Watson for fifty years was cussed and discussed more than any other man in Indiana. But it worked and he managed to serve his country — and incidentally stay on the Federal payroll — for half a century.

(*Congressional Record*. Senate. 78th Congress, 1st Session)

But what, it may be asked, is left of this old-style back-slapping, fraternizing, warmly personal politics in the age of the computer and the public-opinion analyst? An off-the-cuff rejoinder would be to point to the success, locally and in Congress, of a certainly old-style pro, "Tip" O'Neill Jr., Speaker of the House of Representatives and personification of the Boston Irish in politics. But with every year that passes there are fewer "Tip" O'Neills left, and it cannot be denied that the old-style politics of clannishness, patronage, and corruption has found difficulty in keeping pace with changing times. Though the spread of the welfare state may not have destroyed the social justification of the machine, it has sharply reduced the limits of its acceptability. When, undermined in this capacity, the machine still tried to survive in its own purely selfish role, it found the going unexpectedly difficult. The shadier side of Jim Watsonism and its irrelevance to so many of the pressing issues of the '50s and '60s stimulated the rise of an attitude always latent amongst the American public of 'anti-politicism', aversion to the politician as such. Actual corruption apart (and it was seldom apart for long), the elements of bogosity and sham inherent in the system always exposed it to the hazards of public revulsion and revolt. 'Politician' was a label to which was always attached an element of opprobrium, even when not deserved.

Thus it comes about that the American style in politics includes a recurrent reversion to anti-politics; there are votes to be won by running not merely against your opponent, but against politics as such. American history is replete with examples of those whose political careers have taken off from this springboard — Ulysses S. Grant, Woodrow Wilson, Herbert Hoover, Dwight D. Eisenhower, Adlai Stevenson, to name but a few. The campus, in particular, is recurrently called upon to provide some kind of non-political integrity which the party club-house is felt to lack.

Some of this yearning for a non-political politics reflects of course the lack in the American system of provision for non-partisan personifications of national unity. In a system in which the Speaker of the House, the Presiding Officer of the Senate, often the Chief Justice of the Supreme Court, and of course the President of the United States himself are selected as party political figures, there are bound to be periodic hungers for 'supra-party' symbols of the national interest and the national will. This is particularly so when the nation's most obvious problems seem to arise from without, from foreign war or subversion or other causes not readily responsive to the placebos of party programmes.

The decline of the machine and the distrust of party politics as such have opened the way for a relatively novel style in American politics. This is the style not of a region nor of a group. In so far as it has a local embodiment it is West Coast or Californian. Yet it belongs less to a state than to a state of mind, a belief in the infinite plasticity of politics, in the needlessness, harmfulness even, of strong institutional growths, in the peculiar virtue of the spontaneous act, in the reality of the image, the potency of the moral gesture. It is the product of affluence, whereas the old machine politics reflected, if not poverty, at any rate need. Most of its practitioners have arrived, whereas the old machine politicians were still aspiring. They are the products not of the great cities, but of the suburbs and the exurbs. They are more closely linked to the 'opinion industries', education and the media than to the production of goods and services. They inherit the distrust that Americans always feel for 'politics' and 'politicians', and treat parties as intermittently unavoidable inconveniences. More than this, they carry to lengths that Europeans find incredible the traditional American hostility to government as such. Washington they see as a foreign capital; as a centre of power it may have to be taken and occupied, but the occupation should last only as long as the job that has to be done. In desire, if not in fact, they echo the aspirations of the Oregonian Congressman, elected in 1980, who said on his arrival at the Capitol that he wanted his House career to be a "combat tour" — "zoom in, balance the budget and then return to private business". From such a standpoint there is no art, still less any science, of government. There are only self-evident moral or economic truths which have to be translated, as directly as possible, into legislation or executive action. 'Public service', expressed as a career distinct from politics or crusading, gets short shrift; a weak growth in Washington soil at the best of times, it wilts quickly when the emphasis falls so heavily on ideological ends at the expense of utilitarian means. The conviction is pervasive that the reformer (and reform is of the essence of such a politics) must keep himself untainted, either by the lure of permanent office or by the foreign folkways of the

Babylon by the Potomac. Thus emerges the ultimate paradox of Congressmen and Presidents seeking election and even re-election on an appeal not merely of throwing the rascals out, or even of doing away with rascality (i.e. political parties) as such, but of extirpating the very haunts of rascality, of driving government itself out of government. Of course it does not work out quite like that, because real life breaks in, with its urgent problems requiring practical solutions. But a politics of anti-politics makes the search for such solutions that much harder than it need be.

The new politics might be said to have been born of leisure and anxiety, the leisure from the vast productive capacity of post-World War II America, and the anxiety from the burdensome role which that same war placed upon her in every sphere — but most obviously, of course, in Korea and Indo-China — as the Prometheus of atomic fire and the Atlas of the western alliance. To this anxiety the old politics had conspicuously little to say. Technology made its own contribution to these developments by furnishing new powers and refinements of communications and control, television and electronic data-processing. All this came together for the first time in the election of 1952 when television and the large-scale employment of advertising agencies made their first significant impact across the nation. It returned with added power in the '60s and '70s.

Two main varieties of the new politics are discernible. The first, which dominated the seventies, is participatory. The 'children's crusade' that nominated Eugene McCarthy in New Hampshire in 1968 and the students and peace groups who organized for George McGovern in 1972 represented a new source of political manpower to replace the devitalized and shrunken ranks of the ward-heelers. They, and the housewives who joined them, were volunteers with leisure, education, and enthusiasm. But they were also highly principled and selective in their politics, giving allegiance to causes and candidates, but without sustained commitment to party or institution. For such, California, with its cross-filing primaries and its ready resort to the initiative and the referendum, designed, very effectively, to loosen the grip of party almost to vanishing point, was the ideal stamping ground. Here was no party machine to grind down the individualities of its followers, no boss to be obeyed, no historic commitments to group or doctrine that had to be respected. Instead youth, mass participation, and emotional appeal combined with mobility and rootlessness to create an easily aroused but also easily 'turned off' following for a political leader with comparable youth, public charm, and easy access to the media.

In the wake of the participatory manifestation of the new politics — but not necessarily in conflict with it — came the manipula-

tory aspect. Here the key factors are the new instruments of communication — the media — and the newly refined devices of opinion
measurement, derived from the sample poll. Essentially what has
occured here is the application to politics of what David Potter so shrewd-
ly identified as 'the distinctive institution of [American] abundance',
advertising. The techniques for measuring consumer preferences and
suggestibility in the world of retailing have here been applied to the voter.
The early sport of predicting which of the candidates is likely to win has
now developed into an art by which, from the elicited likes and dislikes of
the voter, a candidate may be constructed, and issues and stances supplied,
to create a totality of appeal that can be certified in advance as sure to carry
the day. This at least is the claim of the political-management firms which
now offer their services to candidates or groups belonging to any party, or
to none — services, moreover, which are not confined to election times
but are at the disposal also of incumbents seeking advice on their handling
of public issues. Such professionals are to the old style ward-heelers what
the computerized assembly line is to the rural craftsman. Given enough
money, they can do the job without the old army of pros, or even indeed
without the new cohorts of volunteers. They will locate the areas of
strength and weakness, they will play on them by television commercials
and carefully organized and orchestrated 'happenings', they will construct their data banks and call up their supporters to the polls on election
day. And, of course, having contrived the means, they will then claim a
voice in the ends. From the back room they will move to the council
chamber.

Such are the claims and such, obviously, are the possibilities.
Whether they are the likely actualities is another matter. Just as the
politics of participation, in its non-party form, has failed to display the
capacity for persistence which is the *sine qua non* of any lasting political
success, so the politics of manipulation has perpetually to revise its
claims in the face of human cussedness and irrationality. What has
happened and looks like going on happening is that the new techniques
are superadded to the old. The poll and the TV tube are here to stay; the
measurements and the images are, in their way and up to a point, real
enough. No candidate can afford to ignore them (though many may not be
able to afford to pay for them), but then he cannot afford to ignore the
older techniques either. So the main result is to superimpose additional
burdens of communication, adjustment, and the construction of support
upon the candidate. Flashing a smile on the screen does not replace the
shaking of live hands. Purchasing a commercial does not do away with
the press conference. Renting a crowd is not a substitute for building a
consensus. But what the dedication to such skills may do, of course, is to

distract the people's choice from the job he has been elected to do — to govern. In that task there is still no substitute for personality, loyalty and the ability to sustain a cause with conviction and persistence. In all societies these gifts come rarely and their exercise takes a heavy toll of those who practise them. In American society, mobile, diversified, impatient, and eagerly melioristic, the task is heavier than in most. History records, however, that it has been met and discharged, not unsuccessfully, before. There is no reason to suppose that it has become insuperable now.

NOTES

1. Why, one may ask, has voting turnout declined since television became an integral part of presidential campaigning?
2. Richard F. Fenno, *The President's Cabinet* (Cambridge, Mass.: Harvard University Press, 1959), p. 5.
3. Eisenhower's illness stimulated efforts to make legal provision for Presidential incapacity and in 1967 the twenty-fifth Amendment was ratified providing two methods by which the Vice-President can become Acting President: (a) if the President, in writing, informs Congress of his own incapacity, or (b) if the Vice-President and a majority of the Cabinet or of some 'other body' created by Congress pronounces him so.
4. Slavery indeed may have helped here, not only in the direct Aristotelian sense of providing the leisured base on which a busy public life can rest, but in nourishing a snobbish assumption that alternative modes of employment such as commerce and industry were less worthy of the talents of a gentleman. Finally indeed, as the pressures against slavery mounted, defense of the institution drove Southerners to an even greater exploitation of the political devices which the Constitution provided to enable them to preserve a labor system well after it had been ostracized by the rest of the civilized world.
5. William S. White, *Citadel: The Story of the U.S. Senate* (New York: Harpers, 1956), pp. 67, 69-70.
6. *The Mind of the South* (New York: Alfred Knopf, 1941), p. 130.
7. *The American Irish* (New York: Macmillan Co., 1966), p. 62.

A Good Word for Politicians
by
Charles McDowell

Charles McDowell, Washington columnist for the Richmond Times-Dispatch and a panelist on the PBS program "Washington Week in Review," spoke "in defense of politicians" at the University of Virginia's Fall Convocation 1984. A native of Danville, Ky., he grew up in Lexington, Va., the son of a Washington and Lee University law professor. A graduate of Washington and Lee and the Columbia University Graduate School of Journalism, Mr. McDowell joined the Times-Dispatch in 1949 and has been Washington correspondent and columnist since 1965.

During his visit to Charlottesville, Mr. McDowell received the third Burkett Miller Award from the University's White Burkett Miller Center of Public Affairs. Previous recipients include Jefferson biographer Dumas Malone and Secretary of State George Shultz.

Mr. McDowell was introduced at Fall Convocation as an "astute political observer whose comments always reflect good humor, moderation and good sense." Here are some of the comments he shared with the University audience.

The mission that I invented for myself is to say a good word for politicians — generic politicians — and I can see faces falling all the way back to the Rotunda. Why would anyone want to come out on a beautiful day in October to probably the single most beautiful man-built place on this continent and say a good word about politicians. It just seems gratuitous.

I'll tell you why I'm going to do it, and I feel moderately deeply about it. I think my mission is to remind those of you young enough to accept advice that you really can take pride in the free government that has worked for 200 years and to suggest to you that politicians must have had something to do with it. I would like to encourage you to consider public service, or at least to become involved in political affairs.

Anyway, I'd like for you to be aware enough — to learn e-
nough — to be wary of "anti-politics" as the philosophy of government in
America. By "anti-politics," I mean a moralist, rigid, ideological
approach to government and a contempt for politicians who believe in a
spirit of compromise and consensus as what's necessary to hold a diverse
country together.

The American tradition is reverent toward our free institutions but
skeptical and often contemptuous of the politicians who maintain our institutions. Political humorists built on that contempt. And it's a wholesome skepticism. It's a populist kind of thing — not to really be very
reverent toward our masters of government. That's good stuff. That's
where Mark Twain and Will Rogers came from. What worries me is when
that contempt becomes ritualized and turns into something people take
seriously.

Mark Twain said maybe the meanest and best sentence ever said
about the Congress, which is sort of my college of politicians. He said
"There is no distinctively native American criminal class except Congress," and that sets the tone for much of our comic and even serious
literature. Our newspaper cartoons are founded on the one-joke principle
that politicians are less than ordinarily moral and decent. One can assume
from the Johnny Carsons down through 200 years that politicians
generally are dumb, self-serving, probably crooked, and almost surely
moral illiterates.

Well, I confess that in 30 years or more of trying to cover politics I've
seen some crooks and I've seen some fools. The astonishing thing is relatively how few — enough. As for crooks, reaching for some hope of less
corruption all the time is the history of government in America, for the
last half century, anyway.

And remember, when you think about political corruption, that
political corruption is not something politicians tend to do alone. Consider Watergate. That's about the largest one we ever had. It made Teapot
Dome look pretty petty, because Watergate was constitutional corruption. Nearly two dozen people were convicted and sentenced for serious
crimes in the Watergate scandal, and not one was an elected official. Not
one. These were lawyers, executives, advertising men, public relations
experts, believers in morality in America. It was they who came into a
political campaign and into Washington full of contempt for politics and
politicians, and their contempt for politics and politicians lies at the root
of the Watergate scandal.

One elected politician was involved. His name was Nixon, and he
was not convicted of anything. The heroes of Watergate were politicians — politicians who rose to the occasion as few have in the history of

our country, particularly Republican politicians, who saw constitutional crime for what it was, who had a sense of proportion and morality and outrage and who brought down a corrupt administration.

My own observations of politicians, after 20 years in Washington and 10 in the Virginia legislature:

— Politicians as a profession are at least as honest, intelligent, hard working and morally reliable as the cross-section of doctors, lawyers, business people, union leaders, farmers, college professors, newspaper people or anybody else.

— Politicians as a profession do care about their duty and their country and they particularly care about their constituencies, which I think Mr. Jefferson understood, and I wonder if many of us still do. We elect politicians out of constituencies, and those constituencies vary.

— The good politician comes not only to know his own constituency but to respect the constituency of his opponent and to get some notion of how his opponent's motives tend to lie with that constituency's interests. It's a small matter but an amazing number of people don't care about it.

— The really good politicians, and there are many of them, develop a broader and more enlightened and more compassionate view of our society than most of the rest of us ever do.

Sure there are often times narrow ones, self-righteous ones, and I mentioned fools earlier. But the narrow ones, the self-righteous ones and the simpletons are to some degree self-correcting. They tend not to be effective. They tend not to achieve much influence. They tend not to last as long as the good ones. Those are all tendencies; don't bet on them.

For all I say that is noble about politicians, I have to remind you that a poll shows that people rate politicians among the least trusted professions, down with used car salesmen and news reporters. Polls on the reliability, honesty and competence of Congress show that only about 30 percent of the American people give only a vaguely positive rating to members of Congress as a whole.

But listen to the other side of that. When the same respondents are asked about their own congressmen, 65 to 70 percent give a positive judgment. Even if they don't agree politically with the congressman, they rate him fine for being reliable and reasonably fair minded and not a crook.

So what it shows us is that it is all those other members of Congress who are so bad. It's all those politicians we don't know. They're the ones who are so shameless in voting for special interest legislation and a pork barrel project for the district. Our congressman tends to be pretty good, our mayor, our whatever. It's everybody else's that we just assume are not so hot.

Why are we so hard on politicians? Why do we go beyond what I would consider a healthy skepticism and really warp our view of something that should mean so much to us? I think one thing we do is put down politicians as a way of simplifying our own lives. If you just put the politician down as a fool and a nut and probably an idiot, then you don't have to think about the difficult issues he is dealing with anymore. You don't have to think about democracy itself, if you're willing to put down politicians hard enough.

If we don't put down all politicians, we tend to try to sort them out and label them — the good guys and the bad guys. Now we're learning to say the good women and the bad women. We don't have to judge the issues or understand them at all if we've got everybody sorted out as the good ones and the bad ones, and we're with the good ones!

When was the last time that you remember being with a good one that you thought the other one was other than a bum? Amazingly few people have an election day in their life where they think they are choosing between two good candidates. We flatter ourselves and deceive ourselves by picking the one we like, through our self-interest or through knowing something, and we won't settle for the fact that the other one might also be a very responsible, decent citizen. We ease our minds by saying he or she is a bum, worthless. Another thing we do is commit ourselves to an ideology, a strict set of righteous beliefs that don't allow for another view at all. We make a religion of politics, or to be timely, politics of a religion.

I suggested that anti-politics is on the rise as a philosophy of government in America, and I think it is. Television as the medium of politics probably promotes that phenomenon. TV draws us to personality. TV draws us to impressionistic judgments about leadership. It draws us to a simplistic treatment of complex issues in terms of right and wrong.

Probably it's no coincidence that political parties have lost coherence and influence in the age of television. For more than a century political parties have been the basic mechanism of consensus, compromise and moderation in American politics. Now they are being supplanted, in advocacy and in fund raising, by political action committees devoted to single issues or narrow, hard ideological positions.

Many Americans find it somehow patriotic to brag that they vote for the person and have an inestimable kind of contempt for the parties themselves. I also think that's a sad development.

All of this contributes to the rising theme of anti-politics in American.

The last two presidents — Carter and Reagan — have run against Washington. They have dealt distantly with Congress as if offended by its processes and by its folkways. They have tried to demonstrate that they are not really politicians. That's too bad. For still it's the politicians that have to do the job of balancing competing interests in this country, who have to do the job of promoting great principles through compromise, and who have to do the job of making government work. To make government work, we have to bring majorities together. That requires flexibility. To make government work fairly, and in some hope of true glory, we have to understand the rights of minorities. That requires wisdom and compassion. We are a diverse people, geographically, religiously, ethnically, economically — in other words, politically. We have a thousand factions in this country.

What holds us together in this diversity is nothing more nor less than the practice of politics under a Constitution drawn by politicians. That's the strength of the United States.

The President, Congress and Foreign Policy
by
Kenneth W. Thompson

I was rapporteur and wrote the paper for a recent study of the President and Congress and Foreign Policy that two groups, the Former Members of Congress — 800 former senators or congressmen — and the Atlantic Council in Washington prepared. The study which was based on ten working papers by leading authorities and by extensive discussions in a group which was chaired by Senator Edmund Muskie and Under Secretary of State Kenneth Rush included former Senators Clark, Robert Griffin, Gail McGhee, Hugh Scott, Congressmen Walter Judd, Martha Keys and John Lindsay and Donald McHenry, and Henry Fowler, David Newsom, James Schlesinger, Harold Saunders, Brent Scowcroft, and others from the executive branch. The paper that emerges from such a body obviously bears minimal relationships with the personal convictions of the author; but, in any case, this group was seized with the problem of the relationship of the President and Congress.

What is the relationship between the Executive, our principal subject of concern, and the Congress? This question was debated at the Constitutional Convention. It was resolved in a manner of speaking. Many of the provisions though were vague and uncertain. The living Constitution became something quite different from the written Constitution, at least as some of the founders had conceived it. The debate goes on and will go on because underlining the resolution of that debate is the recognition that neither of the well known positions, namely, executive supremacy or congressional supremacy, have proved acceptable.

You remember that the argument that Alexander Hamilton used in *Federalist No. 6* was that the Executive ought to be responsible for foreign and defense or security policy. Hamilton said, "Are not popular assemblies frequently subject to the impulses of rage, resentment, jealousy, avarice and all the other irregular and violent propensities?"

Thomas Jefferson, more favorable to legislative bodies than Hamilton, argued that the "transaction of business with other nations is executive altogether." Jefferson went on to insist, as had others before him, that the Congress nevertheless had a role.

Others made the case at the Constitutional Convention that Congress ought to be dominant in foreign policy and security policy primarily because it alone was accountable to the people. It was close to the source of the popular will on policy. Unless the people have approved a course of action, that course of action, as we learned in Vietnam and as we have learned throughout our history, would prove unsustainable. Therefore, Congress which held the power of the purse and which had authority to *declare* war — although, it should be noted, not to *make* war — had a role in foreign policy and that was the controversy at the Constitutional Convention. The original proposal was that it should be stated that the Congress had the power to make war. Arrayed against that view was the argument that, in fact, sudden and unforeseen actions required prompt and immediate responses. A body as varied and numerous as the Congress was unlikely to be able to respond with dispatch. If we had any doubt that this was the way crises present themselves, the events of the summer of 1985 ought to have disabused us of that notion. (The TWA hijacking had just occurred.) All too often great crises in foreign and security policy occur without warning in the night and the President or Secretary of State must respond. The President or the Secretary receives a call at two in the morning asking what is the policy of the United States regarding such and such an issue.

Congress has the power to ratify treaties, and, as we saw in the discussion on SALT II, this power can involve the rejection of a program; Congress may exercise an all powerful and dominant role with regard to a national policy that the Executive has actually negotiated. A former Under Secretary of State made the point that only the United States among leading powers at the end of negotiations and the completion of an agreement is unable to assure other nations that the agreement will be approved and sustained by its own government. We stand alone in this regard and we stand alone because two-thirds of the Senate has the power to ratify treaties. So the notion of shared and overlapping powers and a balanced Constitution is uniquely American and British. Note that even John Locke, in his writings on the British system with the emphasis he gave to the primacy of the legislature, nonetheless came down on the side of shared responsibilities. That concept represented the views of the founders.

The philosophical, if not the theological, foundations of this view were expressed by Madison in *Federalist No. 51*. In effect, Madison said,

"If men were gods no government would be necessary. If men were devils no government would be possible." But because men possess nobler as well as lesser virtues and are a curious mixture of good and evil, strength and weakness, a system must be devised which balances lesser motives, and channels nobler motives toward the agreed ends of the nation as a whole. In part for these reasons, a system was established and founded on essentially three streams of experience. The three streams included, first of all, the British experience. The British had themselves merged foreign policy powers and executive and legislative roles. Parliament controlled the purse, but the king managed information and dominated diplomacy. In the 17th and 18th century, the trend was for parliament to increase its power at the king's expense. George III's treatment of the American colonies added to concern in the colonies with excessive executive power. But the British lesson for Americans, whatever one might say about Britain's rulers, was fundamentally a lesson of overlapping, rather than exclusive executive or legislative powers.

The second stream that formed the basis of our experience was colonial practice and history. Again this experience could lead in opposite directions depending upon what weight one gave to a particular experience. On the one hand, there was a dominant hostility toward the executive, whether it was George III, the king, or his royal governor. As a result, by 1776, of the eight states with written constitutions, only New York State opted for executive supremacy. But this practice of weak executives took its toll in some of the original states. It brought uncontrolled disorders like Shea's rebellion and anxiety and frustration for the people. Only in New York were the people spared from certain of these experiences by the existence of a strong government. Hence, the colonial experience offered a mixed lesson just as in the case of the British experience.

The third stream that would lead in the direction of the American constitutional system as it was to evolve were the Articles of Confederation themselves. During the Revolution, General Washington suffered from lack of resources and a Congress powerless to act. Similarly, a weak Congress without taxing power checked by state legislatures and their token executives dramatized the need for a stronger national government. And following the Revolutionary War, the shortcomings of the system became once more apparent in the Continental Congress that could not make treaties or form alliances or maintain order within its boundaries.

These streams and something else led in the direction of the system that we have today. Professor George Quester and others have analyzed the different schools of thought that addressed themselves to this subject in political science. There is one group that puts great emphasis upon the

intention of the founders with regard to congressional powers in foreign
and defense policy. It properly points to Article 1, Section 8. Eighteen of
the powers defined in that article are specifically enumerated and seven of
the eighteen relate to foreign policy. Also, the congressional primacy
people point to the fact that Article 1 comes first. It is clear, therefore, in
the Congress' power of the purse, power of appropriations, power over
treaties, powers defined in Article 1, powers of confirmation of appointments, and declaration of war, that Congress really determines foreign
policy, and that any power that the Executive has is derivative from that.
This is the view of one group of scholars.

The other view points up the fact that the colonial experience and the
Articles of Confederation experience made it clear that the Executive
must be the principal actor in the foreign policy realm. After all the Constitutional Convention opted with very little debate for the role of the
Executive as Commander and Chief, a power which President Roosevelt
was to use in the much debated actions leading up to the destroyer deal
and bases in Iceland and Greenland. These actions were taken not
primarily on the basis of the inherent power of the Executive but rested on
his role as Commander and Chief. Lincoln invoked that power in suspending habeas corpus and raising an army and then had his actions ratified
when the Congress came back in session. Those who defend the primacy
of the Executive also mention the nomination and removal of officers, the
receiving of ambassadors, the negotiation of treaties and the power of
veto.

Almost always when the debate centers on a written document, the
contending schools of thought in the end discover that their opposing
views are settled, if they are settled at all, through political practice. The
living as distinct from the written Constitution has been a product of the
acts of people who exercise these powers. If there had not been a George
Washington, the power of the Executive in foreign and defense policy
would have been something quite different.

Take for instance, treaties. Before the negotiations in 1789 on issues
concerning the Creek Indians, Washington sought to consult in person
with the Senate, asked their advice, appeared in the Senate and was in
effect told the Senate had nothing to tell him. He stormed out of the
Senate never again to enter that body for purposes of advice and consent.
Thereafter, he consulted and negotiated on the arrangements of treaties as
much with members of his Cabinet as with members of the Senate. He
didn't ignore them, but he carried on his discussions with the Senate in
written form. That relationship left its imprint on executive-legislative
relations.

Similarly, if General George C. Marshall had not lived, the pattern of civil military relations and the notion of public service would have been quite different. One thinks of General Marshall as a modern-day George Washington. At the time of the Marshall Plan, someone urged President Truman, who had had some role in its formulation, to use the term Truman Plan. There is some question who conceived the Marshall Plan. It is still discussed in many circles. Some say Harriman, some say Acheson, some say General Marshall; but, the significant thing was that when Truman was urged that the Truman Plan should be the name given to the design for the reconstruction of Europe, he said, "there is only one American whom all other Americans respect and that is General Marshall. We must call it the Marshall Plan." It was similar to the prestige that Washington brought to the office, the quality of leadership he gave, and his determination in propounding a neutrality proclamation in the war between France and England. You recall he was hung in effigy when Citizen Genet organized groups of protesters against him, but Washington's views were sustained and vindicated by history. His action represented an input into the actual living Constitution as did Jefferson's actions with regard to military actions against the Barbary pirates. John Adams notion of "unqualified hostility" is, in a way, the same notion as the notion of undeclared war in Polk's actions in sending troops in the clash between Texas and Mexico protested by Lincoln as a congressman. Later Lincoln himself was to act in ways that he had criticized in the case of President Polk. All of these measures and not least the measures which have occurred in the 20th century helped to shape the executive power in foreign relations.

The period from 1945 to 1965 also helped give form and content to executive leadership in foreign and defense policy. In discussion and debates, men like James Schlesinger argued in Washington, as we prepared our report, that in fact that the period of bipartisanship, which was possible because of the existing consensus on foreign and defense policy, was what he called an island in the sea of contending and shared powers. In other words, the consensus that led to the Marshall Plan, NATO, and the Truman Doctrine, and the other actions which were taken, was made possible because Senator Arthur H. Vandenberg in the Senate, and colleagues like Senator Alben Barkley, Senator Tom Connally, and others, shared a common view of the world and a common notion of what policy should be followed with General Marshall, President Truman, Robert Lovett and with the others who executed policies. Schlesinger argued that these two different functions which one can isolate as defined in the Constitution, namely the making of foreign and defense policy which Congress shares with the President, seemed to merge but only for a brief interval in history. The controversies that sometime divide executive and legislative people was not a gulf which existed in the halcyon days immediately following World War II. You had a consensus and a willingness to accept the recommendations of the Executive with only limited modification in certain amendments proposed in Congress. Then something changed. What was it that changed and why did a change come about?

First of all, the change occurred because of Vietnam and the break-down of the foreign policy consensus. It also changed because of Watergate and the diminution of confidence in the Executive. It changed as a result of a series of forces which had unintended consequences. The religious historian, Herbert Butterfield, liked to write and talk about the unexpected twists and turns of events in history. Actions which were undertaken for one reason had consequences quite different from those that were expected. One such event was the Protestant Reformation which was intended to give the individual, Butterfield argued, the right to interpret the scripture free of any authority outside himself. Butterfield liked to remind us that Reformation led to the immense strengthening of the sovereign power of political units that formerly shared power under a system of the "two swords," the system wherein church and state had divided authority in matters of social and political questions as apart from faith and morals.

Let me try to suggest some of the changes that have come about in the Congress. One of the memories that I have of days in New York is of being told by people like Mr. Robert Lovett, Mr. Dean Rusk and Mr. John McCloy, the people who had been policy makers in the period of the 1940s and 1950s, was that there was no division on either side of the aisle in Congress, especially on committees where questions of the national interest was involved. They also pointed to the fact that executive-legislative relations were strengthened by the fact that often there were sources of knowledge on defense and foreign policy in the Congress superior to that of incoming executive branch elected officials, which would have been understandable, but also to the permanent bureaucracy.

The "juniorization of the Congress" is a phrase that one hears repeatedly. For instance, three quarters of the Senators in the Senate of the United States are new since the beginning of the Nixon administration. The tenure of congressmen and senators has vastly changed. Fifteen percent of the Congress is new every two years. The median tenure of congressmen is four years. Half of the House of Representatives is made up of people who have served six years or less. The median tenure in the Senate has dropped from 10.5 years to 5 years. Nearly a third of the Senate is made up of people who are in their first terms. Decisions have increasingly devolved from the committee level to the subcommittee level. You remember Congressman Sam Rayburn's phrase that "the way to get along within the Congress is to go along." That was the advice which he gave to incoming Congressmen. The maverick legislator was unlikely in this earlier period to emerge as a national figure, someone whose name was identified readily by the public. To advance within that closed system was much more likely if one functioned as a participant in the shaping of policy rather than a critic or an amender or someone who came into prominence by opposing an administration's course of action.

All that has changed today. For one thing, the key committees on foreign and defense policies no longer are made up of people who seek these appointments above and beyond all other appointments. For another thing, the key committees, for instance in the Senate, the Foreign Relations, Armed Services, and Select Intelligence Committee, are broken down into subcommittees, in the Senate four Appropriation subcommittees, six Armed Services subcommittees, seven Foreign Relations subcommittees, and four Intelligence subcommittees. Similarly, seven Armed Services subcommittees exist in the House itself. The number of subcommittee hearings has increased 143% since the early 1970s. The average size of staff has vastly increased. Alan Schick and others in political science have called attention to the profile of staff people emphasizing their upward mobility and quick study traits. I can recall the very strong arguments which executive branch figures like Cyrus Vance used to make when I worked in New York in favor of what they called "a Brookings for Congress." Congress was handicapped in its staffing as compared with the executive branch, the State Department or the Defense Department where you had masses of staff serving. So in response to this, "the Brookings for Congress" idea was designed to produce a vastly increased staff so that now the average staff size for a Senator is 36, for a House of Representative person is 17. The 889 committee staff professionals in general now are matched by 200 foreign policy professionals alone and 252 others that are on a personal staff of Senators who deal somewhere or other with foreign policy issues. The number of amendments put forth in subcommittee has vastly increased. The leaders that we remember who gained public recognition on the Panama Canal Treaty are people like Senator Deconcini of Arizona who offered amendments. The critics in Congress rather than the supporters attracted public attention.

The dominant role of individual Congressmen and the decentralization and diffusion of power in the Congress are factors to contend with in the future. For the foreseeable future, the Congress appears certain to share power with the President in foreign policy. Whether this is a return to the intent of the founders is less important than that future Presidents must assume they will be required to accommodate to the changing pattern of Congressional action. This fact is a reality for foreign policy in the 1980s and 1990s; it imposes still greater demands on those who would bring about new forms of cooperation between the executive and legislative branches.

The President as Commander in Chief

by
Eugene V. Rostow

In any state, the command of the armed forces is the ultimate component of executive power. Article II, adapting British practice, designates the President Commander in Chief both of the nation's armed forces and of the state militia when called into federal service. Article IV, guaranteeing each state a republican form of government, somewhat qualifies that authority. It provides that the national force be used to suppresss domestic violence only on application of the state legislature or of the governor when the state legislature cannot be convened.

I

With regard to domestic (and republican) tranquillity, it became apparent soon after 1789 that the deference of Article IV to states' rights did not permit the national government fully to protect "the peace of the United States." *In re Neagle* (1890). While state governments dealt with most episodes of domestic disorder — and still do — some of these episodes had a national dimension. As early as 1792, Congress declared that "it shall be lawful for the President" to use national troops or call forth the militia whenever he deemed such action necessary to protect the functioning of the government or the enforcement of its laws. President Washington on horse-back leading more than 12,000 national guardsmen to suppress the Whiskey Rebellion of 1793 is the classic symbol of an independent national power to enforce what the President, echoing Rousseau, called "the general will." This power has been invoked regularly, most notably during and after the Civil War, but also in major strikes affecting the national economy, *In re Debs* (1895); the melodrama of *In re Neagle* (1890); and the enforcement of judicial decisions ordering racial desegregation during the 1950s and 1960s. President Taft used the national force to protect Oriental aliens threatened by a local mob, relying only on his duty as President to carry out the international obligation of the United States with regard to aliens.

The formula of the 1792 statute, like that used in later statutes, straddles an unresolved controversy between the President and Congress. Congress insists that its power to pass laws "necessary and proper" to implement the President's authority as Commander in Chief includes the right to restrict the President's capacity to act. All Presidents, on the other hand, while recognizing the necessity for legislation in many situations, claim that statutes cannot subtract from their constitutional duty and power to preserve the Constitution and enforce its laws. *Myers* v. *United States* (1927). While the pattern of usage is by no means uniform, Presidents generally conform to statutes which purport to reinforce and structure the President's use of the armed forces in domestic disorders, at least as a matter of courtesy, unless "sudden and unexpected civil disturbances, disasters, or calamities," in the language of Army regulations, leave no alternative. Some Presidents have even paid lip service to the Posse Comitatus Act (20 Stat. 152 (1878), (18 U.S.C. 1385, 1970), a dubious relic of the end of Reconstruction, which prohibits the use of the Army in suppressing domestic turbulence unless "expressly" authorized, by employing marines for the purpose.

Modern statutes usually retain the ancient requirement of a public proclamation before force is used to restore order, although Presidents sometimes ignore it. The use of force by the President (or by a governor) in dealing with civil disorder does not alone justify suspending the writ of habeas corpus (cross reference). That cannot be done so long as the courts remain capable of carrying out their duties normally. *Ex parte Milligan* (1867).

II

The use of force as an instrument of diplomacy or of war and other extended hostilities does not involve issues of dual sovereignty but has presented significant constitutional conflicts both between Congress and the President, and between individuals and the state. (WAR, FOREIGN AFFAIRS, AND THE CONSTITUTION) The President's power as Commander in Chief under such circumstances goes far beyond the conduct of military operations. It is also the President's prerogative to deploy troops and weapons, at home and abroad in times of peace and war, and to use them when no valid law forbids him to do so. *Little* v *Barreme* (1804). The purposes for which the President may use the armed forces in carrying on the intercourse of the United States with foreign nations are infinite and unpredictable. They include diplomatic ceremony and demonstrations of power; the employment of force, in self-defense in order to deter, anticipate, or defeat armed attack against the interests of the United States or any other act in violation of international law which would justify the use of force in time of peace; and (or) declaring war. In actual hostilities, it is the President's responsibility to negotiate truces, armistices, and cease fires; to direct the negotiation of peace treaties or other international arrangements terminating a condition of war; and to govern foreign territory occupied in the course of hostilities.

These powers are extensive. The use, threat, or hint of force is a frequent element in diplomacy. And military occupations lasted for years during and after the Civil War, the Philippine campaign, a number of Caribbean episodes, and both World Wars. The Cold War has required the apparently permanent deployment abroad of American armed forces on a large scale; novel legal arrangements have developed to organize these activities. While the broad political and prudential discretion of the President and Congress is taken fully into account by the courts in reviewing such exercises of the Commander in Chief's authority, constitutional limits have nonetheless emerged. *Mitchell* v. *Harmony* (1851).

In recent years Congress has effectively employed its appropriation power to qualify the President's discretion as Commander in Chief in conducting military or intelligence operations which were not "public and notorious" general wars under international law. While such contests between the power of the purse and the power of the sword are largely political, they raise the principle of the separation of powers applied in *Chadha* v. *Immigration and Naturalization Service* (1983), WAR, FOREIGN AFFAIRS, AND THE CONSTITUTION. Unless the post-Vietnam Congressional encroachment on the Executive power is reversed, this practice can be expected further to clarify a particularly murky part of the boundary between the executive and the legislative.

PART TWO

Vietnam and the Future

Moral Contradictions or Political Consensus Before and After Vietnam
by
Kenneth W. Thompson

Each era in American foreign policy has confronted new problems. With foreign policy as with the prophet: 'there is no end to trials and tribulations.' The promise of a brave new world has yet to be realized. Our problems intensify as if by an inner logic — one difficulty follows another, one set of issues rolls in in the wake of what was proclaimed to be the final solution to stubborn problems. Basically, each era is foredoomed to its own failures and disillusionments, its illusions and myths. Thus the Wilsonian era was marred by a deep-running misunderstanding concerning the shape the world — its vitalities, its local loyalties, and its strong nationalism. Collective security suffered from an overestimating of the commitments of nations to the international security of the world. Vietnam was a victim of our mistake in underestimating the resolve of a third world power which within its own boundaries had far more staying power than our policy-makers anticipated. As the Secretary of State reported: "The North Vietnamese kept coming." The era of detente may be exaggerating the community of moral and political interests of east and west. The Development Decade or the Year of Europe suffered from a confusion of rhetoric and policy, goals and possibilities, proclamations and achievements. The Reagan Doctrine misunderstands the possibility of intervention in an international system of sovereign states.

What is the root cause of these successive and uninterrupted misunderstandings? Where can one look for the sources of confusion? In facing this question, we tend to attribute the course of history to heroes and devils, mostly devils. If this were true we would be done with the problem once a particular devil (or hero) passed from the scene. However, history teaches that the devil theory has not been very helpful in charting our successes and failures. The main source of the problem is rather the moral contradictions and lack of political consensus existing at any given time whether in the past or future.

Moral contradictions are built into the precepts and practices of the culture. Nor are they confined to foreign policy. They run through American history. We find them repeated by men who have little else in common. It is as if leaders were in the grip of forces they could not control. The fact that we are swept along is not accidental but is inherent in our view of ourselves, of politics and the world. Symptoms and manifestations may vary; the root cause is the same.

Moral pretentiousness is a particular form of moral contradiction. It is more than national egotism. De Tocqueville spoke of American nationalism as a most garrulous and troublesome patriotism.

> If I say to an American that the country he lives in is a fine one, aye, he replies and there is not its equal in the world. If I applaud the freedom its inhabitants enjoy he answers "freedom is a fine thing" but few nations are worthy of it. If I remark on the purity of morals... he declares "I can imagine that a stranger who has witnessed the corruption which prevails in other nations would be astonished at the difference." At length I leave him to contemplation of himself but he returns to the charge and does not desist until he has got me to repeat all I have been saying.

We were God's chosen people and God's New Israel in the new world. With America mankind had reached the culmination of political history. All this is the subject of numerous treatises on nationalism. What is less often noted is the connection between innate moral sentiment and self-justification. It is the first of several contradictions with which we must come to terms. It is not so simply disposed of because it involves the inveterate American custom of joining the search for what is right with the success ethic. Because the American colonists were successful, they were assumed to be righteous.

Americans, said Lincoln, are a people "bereft of faith and terrified by skepticism." We find it hard to live with ambiguity and uncertainty. We can never rest easy with cynicism, even about Watergate. Europeans and Russians were more prepared to accept Watergate as an inevitable deception of politics. Apologists and defenders said that all politicians were corrupt, everyone did it — but somehow for Americans this explanation never carried conviction. The effect on the detente came when the Russians perceived the political consequences within the United States of Watergate. The revolt of the electorate against Watergate reflects a rather stubbornly held American view that it is possible to determine what is right and wrong. Senator Barry Goldwater in his criticism of the

President is more representative of the American ethos than those who defended Nixon. The people are not always sure what is right, but are determined to find out at all costs.

Up to this point, there is no contradiction. Indeed the belief that right can be discovered is oftentimes a peculiarly American strength. The contradiction comes about when righteousness and virtue are identified with power and success. We tend to assume the more successful individual must also be the more virtuous. This is part of our Puritan inheritance. According to this outlook, every rain or drought is due somehow to the virtue or evil of those on whom it falls. The idea of the elect is permanently and indelibly written into the culture: the prominence and prosperity of the select few are outward signs of their being chosen. Writ large, this is the idea of God's chosen people: God made his sun to shine on America. Americans find it hard to live with the idea that we are as other people whether in our strength or our weakness. William James complained that religious people were always lobbying in the court of the Almighty for special favors. They assumed that to pray meant to have their prayers answered precisely as they defined their needs. Reinhold Niebuhr told the story of two early parishioners. The one had tithed since earliest childhood and explained his millionaire's wealth as a result. The other had helped suffering miners with generous credit during their adversity and was bankrupt at the age of 78. Neither of them remembered the Scriptural passage: "for He makes His sun rise on the evil and on the good and sends rain on the just and the unjust." What is wrong with men such as the millionaire is that they seek to explain God's will not in His terms but in their terms. Niebuhr also told the story of the young man who died. His mother and aunt asked why. After a time they answer: "God took him to be with Him because he was so good." An old, worn, and wizened grandfather listened for a long time in silence and finally said "Yes, he was a good boy, a very good boy, but he was not that good." We are endlessly tempted to substitute a fragmentary picture of virtue for God's virtue. We are forever imagining that there are very practical and immediate rewards for being virtuous.

There have been various secular forms of this same outlook, of virtue having its own practical rewards. We have had Dale Carnegies in every period in our history. Secretary of State Stimson declared: "The way to have a friend is to be a friend." More recently from Norman Vincent Peale we have heard about "the power of positive thinking." We also know the refrain: "Love your enemies — so that they will love you."

All these are examples of a rather simple instinct of using religion as a protection against all the insecurities of life. These are innumerable animistic and moralistic concepts of a moral order which rewards the good and punishes the bad. There is no such promise in biblical religion. Biblical morality is closer to the higher morality of which Berdyaev wrote as "the morality beyond morality." "God with us" is a corruption or religious truth. There is no guarantee the righteous will prosper, no assurance the righteous nation will prevail. For the righteous and un-righteous alike live under a morality beyond morality. In that sense, Job is more relevant than Abraham and more sustaining with the burdens we bear or the suffering we endure or the setbacks we experience.

The trouble with moral pretension is that is seeks to close prematurely the great structures of meaning that lie at the heart of the universe, the meaning beyond meaning.

The second moral contradiction has to do with life's tragic element. It is seldom mentioned. In recent days we do not even talk of tragedy. In-deed there is little place for tragedy in dominant nineteenth and twentieth century world views. Surely this was true when the idea of unending progress prevailed. It is also true of the notion that science will save us. The idea of managing our problems or social engineering had no place for tragedy. Compare all these trends with Meinecke's view that "moral life cannot be regulated like clockwork and... even the purest strivings for good can be forced into the most painful choices."

Yet harmonies of interest are less evident than the disharmonies of life. Pundits and popular soothsayers talk endlessly about ways to achieve a natural harmony of interests which they assume is in the nature of things. Quite to the contrary, the evidence is overwhelming that between man and man, man and woman, and nation and nation, the disharmonies of life far outweigh the harmonies. Any thought that men can achieve a simple and easy harmony of interests is almost certain to suffer ship-wreck. Perhaps life would be more tolerable if we recognized the large incidence of disharmonies and braced ourselves to cope with them.

We speak of forgiving one another as God forgives. However, there is no promise that men will forgive one another. The religious idea of God's forgiveness is the annulment of the practical working out of human forgiveness, it too is an expression of the morality beyond morality. The statistics on cooling off periods in divorce are not reassuring; only a tiny fraction of broken marriages are renewed in this period. The concrete forms of realizing such higher moral ends as forgiveness point up the prevalence of the disharmonies of life and the impossibility of achieving the standards of the morality beyond morality or the higher morality.

Similarly, in world politics disharmonies all too often prevail. In the inter-war period, French and British governments came in and out of power, but governments in the two countries with common aims and con-sensus almost never overlapped. Because of this, they failed to concert their policies against Nazi Germany. President Eisenhower and Premier Khrushchev were headed toward a Summit Meeting which might have reduced tensions in the Cold War, only to have the shooting down of the U-2 flight intervene. Secretaries of State Dulles and Rusk were superb negotiators, but because of great power relations in their time they did less serious negotiating than Secretaries with lesser skills. President Nixon's foreign policy opened up American relations with China and the Arabs, but Watergate was his undoing. The Green Revolution raised hope for alleviating famine, but the Energy Crisis has placed the cost of adequate supplies of indispensible fertilizer beyond the reach of many farmers. Advances in civil rights in the early 1960s gave hope, but were followed by a period of benign neglect. The Russian and United States quest for arms agreements came at times when they were unable to complete what each might at another time been willing to accept.

An all too commonplace view has been to see interests as a contradiction of universalism and to cast world order in the form of a substitute for the nation-state. This view may be theoretically right; it is practically unattainable. What is missing is any conception of practical and incremental steps or of how to get from here to there. We talk about new structures of peace — but how are they related to existing structures? The great issue is how to use but not misuse our power, how to recognize our responsibilities within existing structures without opposing constructive change and how to act within the limits of the possible without closing off the future.

Two classic statements throw light on this problem. The one by Tocqueville points up the moral character of the national interest. The other, by Burke, goes beyond national interest to consider its relationship with the interests of others. Tocqueville wrote "the principle of self-interest rightly understood appears... the best suited of all philosophical theories to the wants of the men of our time, and... as their chief remaining security against themselves." There is something tangible and concrete about national interest and specific enough to help men rise above themselves. But self-interest requires that we comprehend more than self-interest, and this is what Burke provided in these words: "Nothing is so fatal to a nation as an extreme of self-partiality, and the total want of consideration of what others will naturally hope or fear." The idea of mutuality of interest is the route by which national interest is transcended. It may be the only route to a new order — ambiguous and uncertain as it is but founded on the solid ground of a decent respect for others. Only through recognizing the self-interest of others is a concern for self-interest saved from itself.

Moral contradictions arise from attitudes of moral pretension, disregard for the element of tragedy in political life, and a too-ready exclusion of the place of national interest and mutuality of interests. We need to keep these factors in view as we approach the post-Vietnam era. They provide a framework for thinking about post-war issues. They link the past with the future and help us to understand the present more clearly.

POLITICAL CONSENSUS

The idea of political consensus arose from the lessons of World War II and the postwar period. However, it may have been premature to claim as universal something which had emerged from our experiences in the 1930's. In the same way, it may have been premature to reject the existing consensus of the 1970s (Mr. Kissinger, for example, declared that the full military alert which was announced at the time of the Arab-Israeli war in 1972 was possible only because the "victim" was Israel). It is said that the only lesson history teaches us is that we learn nothing from history. This is not true — but neither are the examples such as Munich which are advanced as strict analogies to events taking place in the present. Something short of this is possible.

Growing out of our experiences in World Wars I and II, we have gained insights and organized a body of principles on foreign policy that any administration must consider. They are not universal or hard and fast guidelines. They are more in the nature of homely propositions and rules of thumb:

1) Nations need foreign policies. In the nineteenth and twentieth centuries, critics periodically spoke of foreign policies as waste, as something that was expendable. Each day finds America facing new issues and it would be folly to assume we could cope in the absence of a foreign policy.

2) There are limits to foreign policy. It can't remake the world, legislate virtue, or outlaw war or the use of force. Conflicts recur at every hand.

3) Individuals and nations must not tempt thieves. Those who are careless about their security and defense leave themselves vulnerable to aggression. Former Secretary of State Dean Rusk tells a story from his student days in Germany. He hired a canoe but left it on the bank when he went for lunch. When he came out, the boat was gone. He hurried to the police and asked them to arrest the thief. They said "We should rather arrest you for tempting thieves by leaving the boat unguarded."

4) Our national interest requires international cooperation (which in turn has limits). Each nation has its interests and security needs, and this sets limits to international cooperation.

These homely propositions suggest the limits within which we can talk about consensus on foreign policy. Notwithstanding, it is clear there has been a certain breakdown of consensus; we must ask why? What are the implications? How can we account for the loss of confidence in certain basic propositions, such as the adage "don't tempt thieves?" Propositions such as this have been applied in most difficult circumstances across a broad slice of history. In recent months a new situation has arisen. It has familiar characteristics: weariness sets in, fatigue limits action, vitality and stamina run the other way. We learned, despite our national pride and self-righteousness about our allies, that it was the Vietcong and the North Vietnamese who had the best national morale. Furthermore, the crisis occurred in a particular domestic context. It was a period of large-scale student unrest and political instability. All this has contributed and has exaggerated the apparent breakdown of consensus.

There have also been political forces at work within the nation. "Interests never lie," wrote Lord Marlborough. For both critics and opposition, domestic interests came to have primacy over international ones. It became fashionable to say we should return to domestic concerns. It was also a period of unconvincing leadership. Johnson and Nixon should have been effective political leaders, but neither one spoke with authority as time went on.

In ways that it would be difficult to measure, other profound changes were at work. Families known for a stress on discipline and solidarity first encouraged resistance to national authority and then found this resistance being turned against family authority. Religious groups such as the Catholic Church, which had enjoyed unity for centuries, were themselves victims of dissension and division. And not only was dissent all too visible in the society but groups who had fostered non-violence turned to violence to further the goals of dissent.

The Vietnam War also coincided internationally with the contraction of American influence. There was a breakdown of the old order, a decline of old values, a disintegration of old alliances, and the rise of new forces such as the Arab-African bloc. The ties between countries such as Britain and France and the United States were weakened, as they were between China and the USSR in the Communist world system. The Soviet Union moved into the Middle East and the United States opened up relations with China. Existing patterns of international relations were abruptly altered. There was an overturning of idealism expressed in a growing cynicism about international law and international organization, and these years witnessed the decline of the United Nations. The crisis in Korea had given the UN a shot in the arm even as the United Nations gave United States military action in Korea a moral and political legitimacy. With the United Nations decline, a vacuum existed for collective action against aggression.

It was further an era of fragmentation of the political parties. The politics of the Democrats spanned an ideological spectrum from Wallace to Kennedy. The Republicans began with their right-wingers, moved through President Nixon to Senator Charles Percy and beyond. What was common to all these positions was that they had less clearcut views on foreign policy than either Kennedy or Truman, Vandenburg or Eisenhower. While difficult to measure, the play of personalities had a vital and incalculable impact. The hostility between Fulbright and Rusk, Johnson and the intellectuals in and out of government merely illustrate some of the divisions and relationships.

More generally, these years also saw the weakening of the historic political units. The nation-state, the United Nations, and international law — in a curious way all were weakened wherever they stood along the wide range of influence and politics. Finally, there was a shattering of sufficiencies and certainties: of available food reserves in the United States to throw into the balance of crises and famine, of the strength of the US economy, of the stability of the dollar, etc.

To all this must be added an important caveat on talk about consensus. Political consensus within the nation is an ever-changing pattern. The great unanswered question is, "What is public opinion?" We never know what it is until three forces converge: an event, a policy, and a leader. Then there is a further question: Consensus for whom? Nixon made a political triumph out of China. What would have happened to a Democratic President who went to China? Someone must exercise political will before we know what the political consensus is. It has been said that the American people would not tolerate intervention again; yet what about the military alert vs. Russian forces moving into the Middle East? Before the fact it is difficult to know what political consensus is and is not, in general and on a specific issue.

MORAL AND POLITICAL POSITIONS FOR THE POST-VIETNAM ERA

Looking ahead, we know that circumstances affect priorities and values. This is a first principle of a contextual or situational political ethics. The immediate postwar era was one of US supremacy. It was an era of plenty, of money, energy, and will. This was, if you will, situation I. The new era may well be one of scarcity, or situation II. Individuals and nations will need to choose. The answer is not the "Retreat of American Power." Nor was the answer delineated in the Nixon doctrine, which is largely undifferentiated, ad hoc, ill-defined, and has been inconsistently applied.

We need to return to the ancient tradition of moral and political reasoning in thinking about post-Vietnam politics. This is not a task alone for a President and his first minister. In an earlier era, it would have been a responsibility of Policy Planners. In foreign policy, we need a list of do's and don'ts. We cannot do everything. We have to find criteria on which to choose.

We must not assume all our acts will be miraculously blessed and made to succeed. We are virtuous, but not that virtuous. If Vietnam teaches us nothing else, perhaps it will free us of the myth of invincibility. We could live with unresolved and unclarified moral contradictions in an age of abundant resources. They become intolerable in an age of scarcity. For the world into which we are moving we need a sense of the tragic element, of suffering and of the disharmonies and contradictions of life. Otherwise, we move progressively through national and individual psychological stages from utopianism to disillusionment to despair.

We need also to reapply the hard calculus of national interests to ourselves and others. We need to ask what do we need and they need for security rather than trying to psychoanalyze opposing national leaders or engage in the very fashionable and intriguing guessing games: who's up, who's down, who's for war, who's for peace? We may just be entering an era where plain talk may become a political virtue.

It is vital too that we look at the most urgent world problems and ask for which ones do we have something to contribute, to which can we contribute — not all — and for which even if we could contribute would we be allowed to do so. Dr. Bernard Berelson, former President of the Population Council, wrote about the narrowing of possibilities to assist in the less developed countries, and concluded that the only two forms of assistance which will be acceptable in the future are training fellowships and the provision of birth control materials. We will not be allowed to intervene with recipes for family planning or large-scale efforts to change social attitudes. In Northern Nigeria, I was told "thirty years from now we may need contraceptives but today we need clean water."

International security is another urgent problem. Former Secretary of State Dean Rusk has said that nations have rejected collective security but not put anything in its place. Perhaps we need to analyze our past failures and seek lessons for the future. The question is why thorough-going collective security was never used? What lay behind its weakness? Was it the illusions of pactomania? Collective security requires nations to commit for every eventuality but nations no more than individuals can never do this. Secretary of Defense MacNamara spoke of seventy-seven instances of conflict in which nations were engaged in conflict since World War II but the United States intervened in only seven cases. Can we learn why? Secretary of State Kissinger talked twenty years ago of the need for an overall security doctrine, yet today we are no closer or clearer about such a doctrine. We still need more workable and credible concepts. There is need for general principles, not to refute Holmes' dictum that general propositions don't decide concrete cases, but as principles to inter-relate with circumstances.

The problems of the third world in the post-Vietnam era are another vital sphere of concern. On many of them there is little the United States or other outsiders can do. However, we can do more than we are doing. For the less developed countries a massive transfer of capital and people is not the answer, even if this were possible. Outside assistance always tends to be peripheral. The main business for the Secretary of State in the 1980s remains negotiating with the Chinese and Russians, or dealing with great power problems. This fact should serve as a healthy reminder to economic developers that they aren't yet at the center of the world. At the same time, dedicated and concerned policy-makers can in the future with good judgment and common sense, move technical assistance from the periphery somewhat nearer the center. There is something obscene about our officials worrying about great power problems ninety-nine percent of the time and then paying homage to a "new structure of peace" twice a year at the UN. Perhaps this is better than nothing, but it is not much.

An alternate would be to select two or three urgent problem areas, whether agriculture, the environment, or education. Here government could draw on the resources and knowledge of the private sector through questions to those who know. Otherwise this knowledge becomes a wasting asset. We need to ask "How do we go beyond the green revolution?" There is a certain faddism in third world relations. The late president of a great foundation asked his colleagues "What will be my green revolution?" There is need in what we do in the world for more than personal vanity and public relations. In the area of the environment, Maurice Strong recently made a strong plea for help. He spoke of the missing national constituency for the environment. The advances which have been made require public support, including United States support and this is hard, slow, and gradual work — but work which we can under-take now and not in some distant and idyllic future.

There are also possibilities of international cooperation in educa-tion — not self-evident or automatic, and full of uncertainty and possible frustration. In the 1970s an effort was made to discover what programs of higher education for development have succeeded in the less developed countries and if possible why. How can external aid agencies best help education? This effort was supported by twelve of the major donor agencies, international, national, and private. If it had succeeded, it might have been a blueprint for similar efforts in other fields. It illus-trates the kind of modest but practical steps which can be taken. Unhappi-ly, the twelve donor agencies were seized of problems other than educa-tion when the work was completed.

Finally, we live in an era where negotiations are essential. In diplo-macy, there are no miracle workers, for diplomats cannot claim victories if they want to return to negotiate another day. Pride and prestige and their own public opinion drive the loser away. It is a painful business. The period of diplomacy in the 1970s was quite atypical. The Kissinger/Nixon approach to negotiations was not as vital when the United States had an automatic majority. Now others have majorities and we must negotiate sometimes but not always from strength. It is vital that we be clear about the modalities for an era of negotiations which have the best prospect of success. We need to test every method against the circum-stances for its use. It may be that "shuttle diplomacy" introduced a new and vital pattern but equally it may simply have reflected the peculiarities of an immediate situation. The post-Vietnam era will require statesman-ship and wisdom, balance and courage — virtues which can be found in the annals of earlier diplomatic experience. It is to past experience as well as new and forward-looking insights that we must turn. This approach may help free us of some of the moral contradictions from which American policy has suffered. It may also contribute to the building of a more enduring political consensus. The need for clarification is the same before and after Vietnam — it is to reexamine our thinking and the principles which guide our choices.

Seduction by Analogy in Vietnam: the Malaya and Korea Analogies

Yuen Foong Khong

At the beginning of Herzog's *Aguirre the Wrath of God*, a troop of Spanish conquistadors is seen debating about whether to continue the dangerous search for El Dorado. The leader of the expedition urged the troop to turn back but lost out to his assistant Aguirre, who, through argument and intimidation, persuaded the entourage to continue. Aguirre invoked the Mexico analogy twice — Cortez founded Mexico against all odds and survived to reap the fortune — to bolster his argument. What he and his entourage did not know was that El Dorado, that "Lost City of Gold," was a fiction invented by the weak Peruvians to trick them. There was no El Dorado. Only death and destruction awaited them.

Analogies have not played quite so decisive a role in convincing America's leaders to fight communism in Greece, Korea or Vietnam. But they did inform the thinking of successive Presidents, Secretaries, Undersecretaries and others who formulated America's post-war foreign policy. As Paul Kattenburg, former chairman of the Interdepartmental Working Group on Vietnam in the early 1960's, puts it, "Reasoning by historical analogy became a virtual ritual in the United States under Secretaries of State Acheson (1949-52), Dulles (1953-58) and Rusk (1961-68)...." (1980, p.98). Dean Acheson, for example, helped convince Congressional leaders to support Truman's request for $400 million in aid to Greece and Turkey in 1947 by emphasizing the drastic consequences of abdicating this responsibility: like apples in a barrel infected by one rotten one, he prophesized, the corruption of Greece would infect Iran and everything east. Truman's decision to defend South Korea in 1950 was strongly influenced by the lessons of the past. He saw North Korea's actions as analogous to those of Hitler's, Mussolini's and Japan's in the 1930s. These events taught that failure to check aggression early on only brought about a world war later (May, 1973, pp.80-83). If the stakes were so high and the prevention of world war so worthy a goal, it should not come as a surprise that Truman approved MacArthur's march North to roll back totalitarianism (álá Germany and Japan) in the fall of 1950. Four years later, Eisenhower invoked the same analogies to persuade Churchill to join America to prevent the fall of Dien Bien Phu:

> If I may refer again to history; we failed to halt Hirohito, Mussolini and Hitler by not acting in unit and in time. That marked the beginning of many years of stark tragedy and desperate peril. May it not be that our nations have learned something from that lesson?... (cited in Pentagon Papers, 1971, v.1, p.99)

Churchill rejected the analogy; he feared that joint intervention by the United States and Britain "might well bring the world to the verge of a major war" (cited in Schlesinger, 1966, p.7). John F. Kennedy saw great similarities between Malaya and Vietnam — the New Villages of Malaya became Strategic Hamlets in Vietnam, the major difference being the New Villages worked whereas the Strategic Hamlets did not. In meetings with his advisers, Lyndon Johnson repeatedly voiced worries about Chinese intervention álá Korea if the United States pushed Hanoi too hard; United States intelligence then guessed and we now know that it was improbable that the Chinese would have intervened short of a United States invasion of North Vietnam (Pentagon Papers, v.4, p.63; Karnow, 1983, pp. 329, 452-53). More recent and even more dubious uses of analogies include seeing the Nicaraguan contras as the "moral equal of our Founding Fathers," as well as the claim that failure to aid the contras is tantamount to a Munich-like "self-defeating appeasement."

What makes historical analogies so attractive, despite their obvious limitations? I want to argue that historical analogies possess four properties which make them especially endearing to policy makers. One, they explain a new situation to us in terms we are familiar with. This is the "what is" or descriptive property of the analogy. Two, they provide a normative assessment of the situation. This is the "what ought to be" aspect. Three, analogies also prescribe a strategy to get from "what is" to "what ought to be." This is the prescriptive component of the analogy. Four, analogies also suggest what is likely to occur in the future. In other words, they also have predictive abilities. Not all historical analogies exhibit all four characteristics; when they do, however, they become especially potent, and perhaps in the last analysis, mischievous.

I hope to make the above points by examining two of the most important analogies used by policy makers in thinking about Vietnam: Malaya and Korea. Malaya and Korea have also been chosen because they succeed one another as the most important analogies: Malaya being especially relevant from 1961-63, Korea for the crucial years of 1964-66. The structural properties of these two analogies only partially illuminate why they were so popular despite being so imprecise; I am aware that there are cognitive, psychological and historical reasons which also account for their attractiveness. Cognitive explanations, for example, will stress the information processing value of analogies — they allow the policy maker to simplify and assess the vast amount of information out there. Historical-psychological explanations, on the other hand, will stress the degree to which direct experience with the events of the 1930's or 50's conditions policy makers to see future events along those lines. I deal with the cognitive and historical explanations in my research-in-progress; the focus in this paper shall be on the structural properties of analogies.

MALAYA AND THE NEW INSURGENCIES

John F. Kennedy and his New Frontiersmen came into office convinced that China and the Soviet Union formed a monolithic bloc bent on expanding the area under their control. Only containment by the United States — especially in Greece, Turkey and most of all, Korea — have kept the communists at bay. Despite the failure to "integrate" South Korea into the communist bloc, China and the Soviet Union remained inherently expansionist. Their new strategy, however, relied neither on missiles nor conventional troops. "Non-nuclear wars, and sub-limited or guerrilla warfare," Kennedy believed, "have since 1945 constituted the most active and constant threat to Free World security" (Public Papers, 1961, p.229). National Security Action Memorandum 132, signed by Kennedy in Feburary 1962, reiterated this theme. Kennedy directed Fowler Hamilton, the Administrator of the Agency for International Development, to "give utmost attention and emphasis to programs designed to counter Communist indirect aggression, which I regard as a grave threat during the 1960s" (Pentagon Papers, 1971, v.2, p.666). The key word here is indirect, for it was this new communist strategy which called for an appropriate U.S. response.

Kennedy's address to the graduating class of the U.S. Military Academy in the spring of 1962 is worth quoting at length because it spelled out his beliefs more concretely:

> Korea has not been the only battle ground since the end of the Second World War. Men have fought and died in Malaya, in Greece, in the Philippines, in Algeria and Cuba, and Cyprus and almost continuously on the Indo-China Peninsula, No nuclear weapons have been fired. No massive nuclear retalia-

tion has been considered appropriate. This is another type of
war, new in its intensity, ancient in its origin — war by
guerrillas, subversives, insurgents, assassins, war by ambush
instead of by combat; by infiltration, instead of aggression,
seeking victory by eroding and exhausting the enemy instead
of engaging him. It requires in those situations where we must
counter it....a whole new kind of strategy, a wholly different
kind of force, and therefore a new and wholly different kind of
military training (Public Papers, 1962, p.453).

Quite apart from the problem of telling the new graduates that their training might have been obsolete, this speech exemplified the thinking of the
New Frontiersmen. The historian Ernest May found it surprising that
documents of the Vietnam debate in 1961 contained few references to the
Korean analogy whereas documents of 1964 contained many (May, 1973,
p.96). The diagnosis implied in the above speech explains this "surprise":
Malaya, Greece, the Philippines, not Korea, were the models for thinking
about Vietnam in the early 1960s. The Korea analogy illustrated the
aggressive tendencies of communist regimes well but it had one short-
coming. In 1950, North Korea attempted a conventional invasion of the
South; the U.S. U.N. response was also conventional. In 1961-62, the
situation in Vietnam was different. Ngo Dinh Diem's South Vietnam was
not threatened by an outright invasion of regular North Vietnamese units
but by communist guerrillas who were mostly Southerners. Malaya and
the other "indirect aggression" analogies were more useful in explaining
the new kind of war brewing in South Vietnam and in thinking about the
appropriate response to such threats.

The parallels between Malaya and Vietnam are striking. A British
colony until 1957, Malaya was occupied by the Japanese during the
Second World War. The Malayan Communist Party, reorganized as the
Malayan People's Anti-Japanese Army (MPAJA) was the only domestic
group to cooperate with the British to mount an armed resistance against
the Japanese. MPAJA members, mostly ethnic Chinese, mounted
guerrilla operations against the Japanese army. Although they succeeded
in making life difficult for the Japanese, they were unable to dislodge
them.

The MPAJA, however, attracted a substantial number of recruits and
with their anti-imperialists credentials enhanced towards the end of the
war, they emerged as a viable contender for power after Japan's surrender.
Unlike Ho Chi Minh's Communist Party which took over Hanoi in the
aftermath of Japan's defeat, the communists in Malaya did not or were
unable to take over. While they did enjoy some support from Chinese
peasants and workers, they did not really command the support of most

Malays, the majority group in Malaya. When the British returned to Malaya, they quickly and ruthlessly surpressed the communist and the urban organizations (e.g. trade unions) controlled by them. Fighting for their political survival and also reasoning that they did not fight against an imperialist power only to bring back another, the Malayan Communist Party launched a major insurrection in 1948. The insurrection began with the ambush-murder of three European rubber estate managers; assassinations of government officials, terrorizing of uncooperative peasants — the kind of violence which Kennedy alluded to above — were common. The conflict dragged on for twelve years but in the end the guerrillas lost (Short, 1975).

Robert K.G. Thompson is the man most often credited for defeating the guerrillas in Malaya. Initially, the British saw the insurrection as a military problem. They launched large-scale military operations and bombed suspected jungle bases. Two years later, they were worse off than when they began (Hilsman, p.429). Thompson concluded that so long as the guerrillas had the support — voluntary or involuntary — of the peasants, it was impossible to defeat them. He came up with the idea of "New Villages," secure hamlets where the peasants were isolated from the guerrillas. Civic action teams would visit to provide simple government services and the police would train the peasants in the use of firearms and win their confidence so that the communist sympathizers could be identified. The switch from a "search and destroy" strategy to a "clear and hold" strategy contributed greatly to the successful containment of communism in Malaya.

The Malaya analogy is helpful in making sense of the war in South Vietnam. Those familiar with the case of Malaya can identify similar forces at work: a legitimate government, supported by the majority, is threatened by local communist insurgents bent on seizing power at the behest of China and the Soviet Union. Related to, but distinct from, this description is a normative assessment of the parties in conflict in Malaya-South Vietnam: the cause of the guerrillas is unjust, as are the means — infiltration, assassination, terror — they employ. As such, the guerrillas ought to be defeated in South Vietnam as they were defeated in Malaya.

But the Malaya analogy does more than designate the end of defeating the communist guerrillas as good. It also prescribes a morally acceptable means of countering indirect aggression. By morally acceptable I mean a proportional response. In moral discourse, it is not enough to have a moral end, the means chosen to realize that end must also not incur disproportionate costs relative to the benefits conferred by achieving the end. In other words, a just end can be tarnished by unjust — i.e. disproportionate — means.

The proportional response suggested by the Malaya analogy is the construction of New Villages to physically isolate the guerrilla's potential supporters from the guerrillas. As conceived and executed by Robert K.G. Thompson in Malaya, this response to guerrilla insurgency passes the proportionality test because it leaves the rest of the population in peace and the costs of relocation are imposed on likely supporters. Weighed against the end of preserving a government supported by the majority, the costs do not appear disproportionate. The Kennedy administration encouraged Diem to follow this strategy and provided much of the material (Strategic Hamlet Kits) and money necessary to construct the Strategic Hamlets. It is of course not possible to say that Kennedy and his advisers (especially Roger Hilsman) believed in the Strategic Hamlet program because it was morally sound but it is possible to say that the Malaya analogy did not prescribe a strategy which might have exacted disproportionate costs. The idea of proportional response, with or without its moral dimension, would have appealed to the Kennedy administration. It fitted right in with the strategy of "flexible response," the attempt by Kennedy and his advisers to tailor the amount of force the U.S. should apply to the requirements of any given situation.

The Malaya analogy went beyond prescribing a proportional response, it also suggested that such a response could work. Again, in moral discourse, effectiveness is a critical consideration. Pursuing the most noble goal does not make one's actions morally sound if they are unlikely to achieve the goals. The Malaya analogy predicts a high probability of success: if the problem in Vietnam is like the problem in Malaya and if the New Villages worked in Malaya, then they or their equivalent — the Strategic Hamlets — are likely to work in South Vietnam as well. Thus Roger Hilsman, Assistant Secretary for Far Eastern Affairs, believed that the best way to "pull the teeth of the Viet Cong terrorist campaign" was not by killing them but by protecting the peasants in Strategic Hamlets. "[T]his technique," according to Hilsman, "was used successfully in Malaya against the Communist movement there" (*Department of State Bulletin*, July 8, 1963, p.44). By suggesting that the prescribed means is able to attain the desired end (defeating the communist guerrillas), the predictive component of the Malaya analogy reinforces the normative weight of Kennedy's policy towards South Vietnam.

KOREA AND THE CHANGING CHARACTER OF THE VIETNAM WAR

By 1965 Malaya was no longer the dominant analogy. Its place was taken by the Korea analogy. The descriptive, normative, prescriptive and predictive elements found in the Malaya analogy are also present in the Korea analogy.

The Korea analogy was invoked primarily to show that the war in Vietnam was a war of aggression by the North against the South. This is in contrast to the Malaya analogy, which, while implying external support, saw the war primarily in terms of Southern guerrillas fighting against the army of South Vietnam (ARVN). The Korean analogy emphasized the more prominent role, if not the direct participation, of North Vietnamese soldiers. Thus Secretary of State Dean Rusk equated the infiltration of North Vietnamese material and men into South Vietnam with the overt aggression of North Korea against South Korea (*DOSB*, June 28, 1965, p.1032). Lyndon Johnson did the same in his public speeches as well as his private conversations. Years after the he made the fateful decisions of 1965, Johnson admonished Doris Kearns, his biographer, for seeing the Vietnam conflict as a civil war:

> How…can you… say that South Vietnam is not a separate country with a traditionally recognized boundary?….Oh sure, there were some Koreans in both North and South Korea who believed their country was one country, yet was there any doubt that North Korean aggression took place? (Kearns, 1976, p.328)

For William Bundy, perhaps the most consistent proponent of the Korea analogy, Korea forced the relearning of the lessons of the 1930s — "aggression of any sort must be met early and head-on or it will be met later and in tougher circumstances" (*DOSB*, February 8, 1965, p.168). Adlai Stevenson's United Nation address titled "Aggression from the North" best captures the Johnson administration's position. Stevenson, reversing Kennedy's slighting of the Korea analogy, questioned the relevance of the Malaya, Greece and Philippine analogies and went on to emphasize the parallel between Vietnam and Korea: "North Vietnam's commitment to seize control of the South is no less total than was the commitment of the regime in North Korea in 1950" (*DOSB*, March 22 1965, p.404).

What is interesting about the descriptive component of the Korea analogy is that it does provide a better description of "what is" in 1964-66. By the fall of 1964, the U.S. was finding "more and more 'bona fide' North Vietnamese soldiers among the infiltrees" (Pentagon Papers, v.3, p.207). An estimated ten thousand North Vietnamese troops went South in 1964 (Pentagon Papers, v.3, p.207; Cf. Karnow, 1983, p.334). As the perceived and actual nature of the war changed from guerrilla warfare to a mixture of guerrilla as well as conventional assaults, there was also a shift from reliance on the Malaya to the Korea analogy. Both the Malaya and Korea analogies explained the nature of the Vietnam conflict in terms we are familiar with; the Korea analogy, however, captured the changing nature of the conflict more successfully.

If one accepts the description of the North-South relationship — i.e. a case of the North trying to conquer the South — given by the Korea analogy, the actions of the North clearly become unjustifiable. Regardless of how it is put, the normative invocation is clear: aggression ought to be stopped, South Vietnam should not be allowed to fall, the United States ought to come to the help of the South.

The Korea analogy does more than merely invoke these normative ends, it also prescribes the means to realize them: through the introduction of U.S. troops. I am not claiming that when policy makers relied on the Korea analogy throughout 1965 in thinking about Vietnam, they were decisively influenced by the Korean strategy of using U.S. troops to halt aggression. However, if one believes that the problem in Vietnam is like the problem in Korea 1950, one is likely to consider quite seriously the ready-made answer supplied by the Korea analogy, namely, the introduction of U.S. troops. In this sense, the introduction of U.S. ground forces as the appropriate response is part and parcel of the Korea analogy.

Like the Malaya analogy, the Korea analogy also prescribed a proportional response. That is, if one accepts the description, provided by the Korea analogy, that the North was attacking the South. Introducing U.S. troops is proportional in the sense that it falls short of more drastic measures (e.g. invading North Vietnam or using nuclear weapons, see Pentagon Papers, v.3, p.623) and it is a step beyond merely advising and training the ARVN. If Kennedy's interest in not replying with overwhelming force had to do with the dictates of flexible response and the attempt to calibrate force to meet a given threat, Johnson's reluctance to consider a vastly disproportionate response had to do with the fear of bringing about a general war.

Evidence of Johnson's concern about proportionality can be found in a crucial meeting he had with his Joint Chiefs in July 1965, a few days before his decision to grant McNamara's request for 100 thousand combat troops. Johnson probed the JCS for North Vietnamese and Chinese reactions to the proposed U.S. action. The President was worried: "If we come in with hundreds of thousands of men and billions of dollars, won't this cause China and Russia to come in?" General Johnson, Army Chief of Staff, replied that they would not, to which Johnson retorted: "MacArthur didn't think they would come in either" (cited in Berman, 1982, pp.117-18). It is well known that Johnson was always careful about not going beyond like MacArthur did. Consequently the use of nuclear weapons, the invasion of North Vietnam, destruction of the latter's dyke system and bombing the North Vietnamese civilians were never even proposed (Gelb and Betts, 1979, pp.264-65).

Beyond proportionality is the issue of likelihood of success. Here again, the Korea analogy, like the Malaya and virtually all analogies used in thinking about Vietnam, predicts a high probability of success. If the problem in Korea and Vietnam are essentially similar, it stands to reason that the strategy which proved ultimately successful in Korea, namely U.S. intervention, will also be successful in Vietnam. And probability of success, we have argued earlier, adds moral weight to the policy. By providing an optimistic prediction of the likely outcome of introducing U.S. troops, the Korea analogy makes this policy prescription all the more attractive.

MALAYA, KOREA AND VIETNAM: THE IGNORED DIFFERENCES

Having explored the features of the Malaya and Korea analogies which made them attractive to policy makers, it is necessary to point out that there were those who were suspicious of these analogies, in part and in whole. General L.L. Lemnitzer, Chairman of the Joint Chiefs of Staff in the first two years of Kennedy's administration, was highly skeptical of the Malaya analogy. In a memorandum to General Maxwell Taylor, Kennedy's handpicked personal adviser and soon-to-be successor to Lemnitzer, the latter complained that "The success of the counter-terrorist police organization in Malaya has had considerable impact" on the Kennedy administration's approach to Vietnam. Given the "considerable impact" of the Malaya analogy, General Lemnitzer felt obliged to point out its defects. He pointed to five "major differences between the situations in Malaya and South Vietnam." His analysis is prescient and important enough to be cited in full:

a. Malayan borders were far more controllable in that Thailand cooperated in refusing the Communists an operational safe haven.
b. The racial characteristics of the Chinese insurgents in Malaya made identification and segregation a relatively simple matter as compared to the situation in Vietnam where the Viet Cong cannot be distinguished from the loyal citizen.
c. The scarcity of food in Malaya versus the relative plenty in South Vietnam made the denial of food to the Communist guerrillas a far more important and readily usable weapon in Malaya.

   d. Most importantly, in Malaya the British were in actual command, with all of the obvious advantages this entails, and used highly trained Commonwealth troops.

   e. Finally, it took the British nearly 12 years to defeat an insurgency which was less strong than the one in South Vietnam. (Pentagon Papers, v.2, p.650).

Lemnitzer's critique of the Malaya analogy is interesting because it appreciated the on-the-ground differences between Malaya and South Vietnam. He took issue with the description, prescription and prediction provided by the Malaya analogy. The latter implied that sanctuaries for the guerrillas was not a major issue, Lemnitzer believed that such a description did not conform to the situation in South Vietnam, where the guerrillas could have "safe haven[s]" in Laos and Cambodia. Lemnitzer also found the prescription — emphasis on counter-terrorist police and hence political measures instead of emphasis on military measures — suggested the Malaya analogy wanting. He preferred the Philippine experience, where "the military framework used was highly successful" (Pentagon Papers, v.2, p.650). Finally, Lemnitzer was less sanguine about the prediction of eventual success than Kennedy's civilian advisers. The implication of Lemnitzer's analysis was that the Vietnamese communists would be hard to beat.

History proved Lemnitzer right. Even with American troops and command, the National Liberation Front could not be subdued. Uncontrollable borders, namely sanctuaries and infiltration routes in Laos and Cambodia, also partially explain the difficulty. So does the difficulty of distinguishing loyal from disloyal peasants in Vietnam. There was also the character of the government being helped, a crucial difference omitted in Lemnitzer's analysis. Malaya had a relatively stable and popular government both as a British colony and as a newly independent country; it was apparent even by 1961 that the South Vietnamese government was neither popular nor stable. Within the Diem regime, there was constant infighting and jockeying for power, so much so that the only principals Diem could trust were his brothers and their wives; without, Diem did not encourage the setting up of institutions which could have channeled the political participation of the religious sects, nationalist political parties and students.

The other interesting point about Lemnitzer's critique is that it was ignored. The Kennedy administration continued to believe in the relevance of the Malaya analogy. Thus in April 1963, U. Alexis Johnson, Deputy Under Secretary of State suggested that the post war insurgencies in Burma, Indonesia, Malaya, Indochina and the Philippines were coordinated by China but singled out Malaya as the struggle which "provided valuable lessons which are now being applied in Viet-Nam" (*DOSB*, April 29, 1963, p.636). Similarly, Roger Hilsman, Kennedy's major adviser on communist insurgencies, claimed that the best way to defeat the Viet Cong was not by killing them but by protecting them in strategic hamlets, a "technique used successfully in Malaya against the Communist movement there." (*DOSB*, July 8, 1963, p.44)

The Strategic Hamlet program failed. Formally initiated as "Operation SUNRISE" in Bin Duong Province in early 1962, it died with the Ngos in late 1963. The failure of the strategic hamlet does not necessarily mean that the error lay in misapplying the lessons of Malaya to Vietnam but it does make the analogy suspect. It is, however, always necessary to point out the differences which account for the dissimilar outcomes. General Lemnitzer's memorandum — written in late 1961 — is a first step in this direction. To be sure Lemnitzer was not addressing himself to the Strategic Hamlet program, but his observations, if correct, could help explain why a similar program was successful in Malaya but not in Vietnam.

The Korea analogy, on the other hand, found its antagonist in George Ball, Under Secretary of State. In an October 1964 memorandum to Dean Rusk, Robert McNamara and McGeorge Bundy, Ball sought to question "the assumptions of our Viet-Nam policy," before deciding in "the next few weeks" between a number of options, including bombing North Vietnam and introducing substantial U.S. ground forces in South Vietnam (Ball, Atlantic Monthly, July 1972, p.36). Ball wrote:

> ....I want to emphasize one key point at the outset: The problem of South Viet-Nam is *sui generis*. South Vietnam is not Korea, and in making fundamental decisions it would be a mistake for us to rely too heavily on the Korean analogy (Ball, 1972, p.37).

Ball, like Lemnitzer, found five differences. Most of them, in this memorandum at least, dealt with the descriptive deficiencies of the Korean analogy: the U.S. had a clear United Nations mandate in Korea but not in South Vietnam; fifty-three other countries provided troops to fight in Korea while the U.S. was "going it alone" in Vietnam. More importantly, Syngman Rhee's government was stable and enjoyed wide support whereas South Vietnam was charaterized by "governmental chaos." Perhaps the most important difference Ball identified was over the nature of the war: the Korean War was a classical case of invasion whereas in South Vietnam "there has been no invasion — only slow infiltration.... The Viet Cong insurgency does have substantial indigenous support" (Ball, 1972, p.37). Whether Ball intended it or not, and I think he intended it, spelling out these differences raises questions about the normative assessment as well as the predictions provided by the Korean analogy. If the insurgency enjoyed substantial support and if the South Vietnamese government was incompetent, should and could the South Vietnamese regime be preserved?

Ball received better treatment from his superiors than Lemnitzer did from his. After reading the memorandum, Rusk, McNamara and Bundy debated the arguments with Ball on two successive Saturday afternoons (Atlantic Monthly, July 1972, p.33). Ball failed to convince his superiors. The lessons of Korea continued to haunt the principal policy makers, almost to a man. Johnson could not forget "the withdrawal of our forces from South Korea and then our immediate reaction to the Communist aggression of 1950" and he worried about "repeating the same sharp reversal" in Vietnam (Johnson, 1971, p.152). For Dean Rusk, the war in Vietnam, like Korea, was not a civil war but a case of aggression of one state aggainst another across national boundaries (Graff, 1970, p.136). William Bundy argued that it took a war to beat back aggression in Korea and that it might take another to beat back the North Vietnamese and Chinese in Southeast Asia (*DOSB*, June 21, 1965).

If in retrospect some of Lyman Lemnitzer's and George Ball's objections to the Malaya and Korea analogy seem prescient and sound, one needs to remember that their advice was heard but not taken. This was so partly because the descriptive, normative, prescriptive and predictive components of the respective analogies combined to form an internally consistent and remarkably wholesome way to look at Vietnam. Together with the cognitive and historical-psychological reasons alluded to earlier but not discussed in this paper, these structural properties of historical analogies help explain why policy makers hold on to their analogies despite warnings about their limitations.

REFERENCES

Ball, George. "Top Secret: The Prophecy the President Rejected."
    Atlantic Monthly, July 1972.
Berman, Larry. *Planning A Tragedy*. New York: W.W. Norton, 1982.
Gelb, Leslie and Betts, Richard. *The Irony of Vietnam:*
    The System Worked. Washington D.C.: Brookings, 1979.
Hilsman, Roger. *To Move A Nation*. New York: Doubleday, 1967.
Karnow, Stanley. *Vietnam: A History*. New York: Viking, 1983.
Kattenburg, Paul. *The Vietnam Trauma*. New Jersey: Transaction, 1980.
Kearns, Doris. *Lyndon Johnson and the American Dream*. New York:
    Harper and Row, 1976.

May, Ernest. *Lessons of the Past: The Use and Misuse of History in American Foreign Policy.* New York: Oxford, 1973.

The Pentagon Papers: The Defense Department History of United States Decision Making on Vietnam. Senator Gravel edition. v.1-4. Boston: Beacon Press, 1971.

Public Papers of the Presidents: John F. Kennedy.

Public Papers of the Presidents: Lyndon B. Johnson.

Schlesinger, Arthur. *The Bitter Heritage: Vietnam and American Democracy 1941-1966.* Boston: Houghton Mifflin, 1966.

Short, Anthony. *The Communist Insurrection in Malaya 1948-1960.* London: Frederick Muller, 1975.

United States Department of State. *Department of State Bulletin.* 1961-1966.

Persistent Patterns in International Politics: Power, Ethics, and Statesmanship

Nicolai N. Petro and Kenneth W. Thompson

One persistent pattern in international politics involves the relationship between power and ethics. Nations seek power in order to achieve national security and justify their actions in terms of ethical principles. However patterns change depending on the relative power or powerlessness of a given nation and the historic values it seeks to invoke.

The first part of the paper seeks to establish a theoretical framework for examining various patterns in the relationship of ethics and power. We intend to focus on several case studies that will illuminate the changing patterns subsumed under our theoretical framework.

The second part of the paper discusses the persistent patterns of conflict between notions of power and ethics and the responsibilities of statesmen by examining the opportunities for humanitarian intercession in American diplomacy. The domestic debates over the propriety of such intercession show a consistent consensus among public leaders on the need to separate private from public morality during the republic's first century.

A change in this consensus was forged by the combination of America's undeniable strength and the adoption, first by President Wilson and subsequently by Franklin D. Roosevelt, of global responsibilities for the nation. A fundamental part of this emergent consensus is the notion that our global role ought to be morally justified. As a result, the barrier which earlier Presidents placed between individual morality and the morality of states has eroded to the degree that today we can speak of two traditions in American diplomacy: one argues for active intervention in world affairs as a moral duty; the other argues for American self-limitation, again, as a moral good.

As we face the closing of this century, it is appropriate to take stock of the differences in these two approaches to American involvement in world affairs and to discuss their relative problems and merits.

I

Throughout the history of American foreign policy and of writings on international relations, two schools of thought have sought to explain the relationship between ethics and power. One school has reflected the anguish of sensitive minds with the harsh realities of world politics. Its answer has been to substitute moral principles for the stern requirements of maintaining equilibrium in the international system. President Wilson offered his "fourteen points," as a substitute for the postwar territorial settlements which European leaders sought and new viable economic relations required by the Balkanization of Eastern and Central Europe. Lesser philosophers of statecraft than Wilson have chosen to defend not fourteen points but a single moral and political principle as the rationale for peace. The tendency of introducing a single moral principle as a remedy to all the ills of international politics is moralism. Following World War I and II the League and the United Nations were heralded as harbingers of a brave new world. The Pact of Paris sought peace through the outlawry of war. Collective security was seen as a replacement for the traditional alliance system. On returning from the Moscow Conference, Cordell Hull announced that the United Nations, the groundwork for which had been laid at the conference, would mean the end of power politics and usher in a new era of collaboration. Humanitarianism with roots in the philosophy of the Enlightenment and the political theory of liberalism postulated respect for human life and the promotion of human welfare. The major political and social reforms within states of the nineteenth and twentieth centuries were inspired by humanitarianism. Both the efforts in the late nineteenth and early twentieth centuries to make war more humane and the human rights movement in the postwar period owe allegiance to humanitarianism. The League and the U.N., the outlawry of war and human rights, at least in some of their manifestations, are examples of moralism in world politics.

If moralism seeks to relate ethics and power by imposing a single moral principle on the recurrent problems of world politics, practical morality provides guidance through seeking to reconcile the dictates of ethics and power. It recognizes the inevitable tension between moral precepts and the requirements of successful political action. "It is unwilling," to quote one authority, "to obliterate that tension...by making it appear as though the stark facts of politics were morally more satisfying than they actually are, and the moral law less exacting than it actually is." This school of thought recognizes that moral principles can be realized only within an international system which fundamentally has been the same with regard to the location of sovereignty since the Treaty of Westphalia. Thus the worthy principles of human rights must be realized not in terms of their abstract universal formulation but as they are filtered through individual nation states. Not human rights in general but human rights realizable with Korea or the Soviet Union or South Africa or Poland are the focus for practical morality.

The two prevailing schools of thought lead in different directions in the conduct of foreign policy. Moralism oftentimes leads to a crusading posture for policymakers. It defends intervention in the domestic affairs of other states based on one or the other moral principle. The public human rights movement is only the most recent example of this approach. Collective security assumes that turning back aggression can be the paramount foreign policy aim of all peace loving states. The authors of the pact to outlaw war believed that all states dedicated to peace would eschew war whatever their national aspirations or strategic interests might be. If some renegade state or group resisted the moral claim of collective security or human rights, it would be the duty of the international community to intervene to enforce such moral commands.

The other school would reserve decisions about intervention to the specific time and place. It is guided by the principle that what is morally desirable must be balanced against what is politically possible. It prefers to answer the question about intervention not once and for all but in each specific case. It repudiates such absolutist judgments as those contained in the Pact of Paris. Intervention when it occurs must be based on national interest and threats to a given political equilibrium. If those who championed collective security at the end of World War II had recognized such limitations, the disillusionment which has set in about collective security might have been less far-reaching.

Whatever one's views about these historical examples, there is merit in focusing on humanitarianism and human rights within the context of American foreign policy. Such an inquiry may help to illuminate the possibilities and limitations of the two schools of thought. It may bring us closer to an understanding of the relationship in practice of ethics and power for modern statesmen in international politics.

II

Concern for the rights of the individual, so fervently expressed in our founding documents, conflicted with the weakness of the new nation during its first century of existence. Torn between the conflicting aspirations of self-preservation and, as Thomas Paine put it, our obligation "to make the world anew," the Republic's early statesmen generally chose the principle of non-interference in the domestic affairs of others, hoping thus to avoid foreign intervention in our own domestic affairs.

The choices that had to be made were difficult and often unpopular ones for public officials. During this era of upheavals, the suppressed peoples of Europe and Latin America clamored for independence. Revolutionaries proclaimed aloud the principles of humanism, egalitarianism, and nationalism. Many cited the United States as their model and called upon Americans to intercede in support of the ideals they spawned. The arguments made in Congress for and against intercession in many ways echo today's debates over human rights and humanitarian assistance.

The relative weakness of the newly independent colonies, however, seemed to many of the Founding Fathers reason enough to take a narrow and strictly national interpretation of the ideals of the Declaration. Their vision of America was perhaps best expressed by George Washington, when he wrote that America deserved special protection as "an asylum for those who love liberty" in a cause "esteemed the cause of all mankind."[1] Washington felt that the best service America could render to the world was that of self-preservation; to serve as an example for future generations. Not only were the humanitarian objectives a domestic, rather than transnational goal but, they warned, espousing them too ardently might even have a pernicious effect. John Quincy Adams writing in 1780 warned, "not even Spain nor France wishes to see America rise very fast to power. We ought, therefore, to be cautious how we magnify our ideas and exaggerate our expressions of the generosity and magnanimity of these powers."[2]

The first clear expression of America's circumspection in acting in support of humanitarian principles abroad came during Latin America's struggle for independence. Not only did President Monroe delay recognition until *de facto* independence had been established; he went out of his way to indicate that the delay and circumspection with which the United States continued to observe Spanish rights in the area.[3] When, a few years later, Edward Everett, editor of the *North American Review* launched a committee to gather funds to support the Greek insurrection of 1821 and with the press nearly unanimously extolling the efforts of the "heroic" Hellenes against "the savage and barbarous Turk," Secretary Adams dismissed these efforts as "all sentiment." Thomas Jefferson, the retired senior statesman, elegantly sidestepped Greek Scholar Adamantios

Koraes' appeal for help, advising the Greeks to consider for their own use the Constitution of the United States as "a tribute rendered to the names of your Homer, your Demosthenes, and the splendid constellation of sages and heroes, whose blood is still flowing in your veins."[4] As to concrete assistance, Jefferson assured Koraes, "nothing...but the fundamental principle of our government never to entangle us with the broils of Europe could restrain our generous youth from taking some part in this holy cause." These early debates, however, were only a prelude to the first major test of America's committed non-involvement in world affairs — the Hungarian revolt of 1848.

In 1848, Hungarian revolutionaries, led by the flamboyant Louis Kossuth succeeded in establishing their autonomy from Austria. In desperation the Austrians appealed to Tsar Nicholas I to send troops to quell the revolt. The Tsar complied and Kossuth was forced to flee, eventually winding up in the United States where he was showered with honors and worked actively to enlist American support for the liberation of his homeland.

Popular opinion in this country strongly favored the insurgents and in 1849 President Zachary Taylor sent a special envoy to the area to grant recognition if the rebels appeared capable of maintaining their independence. Though this attempt floundered, the Congress and the press continued to debate America's obligation to defend democratic principles around the world, as well as the propriety of Kossuth's appeals.

The pro-interventionists, led by Senators Cass, Seward, and Clarke, argued for a posture of stern moral condemnations of the Russian intervention. Since no sanctions of either Austria or Russia were demanded or expected, they argued that no irreparable harm to our relations with these nations would be done. To the objections raised by other senators and unenforceable protests were worse than futile — they carried the imprimatur of the Congress and of the President of the United States and showed them up to be meaningless — Cass replied by citing Lord Palmerston:

> ...opinions are stronger than armies. Opinions, if they are founded in truth and justice, will in the end prevail against the bayonets of infantry, the fire of artillery, and the charges of cavalry....
>
> That, armed with opinion, if that opinion is pronounced with truth and justice, we are indeed strong, and in the end likely to prevail.[5]

The senators in opposition like Cooper, Jones, and Clemens, most of whom were from the South, argued against intercession on the ground that it was contrary to the conventions of international law upholding sovereignty. It would yield no conceivable advantage, yet succeed in making the United States appear both powerless and foolish. furthermore, once such a policy was begun, they argued, it would have no logical conclusion. To be consistent one would have to indict nearly every nation.

But most importantly, perhaps, for these senators, such a policy of humanitarian intervention contradicted the tradition of U.S. foreign policy. They cited numerous passages from Washington, Madison and Monroe to Andrew Jackson who, Clemens felt, had summarized the national tradition in his fourth annual address to the Congress:

> In the view I have given of our connection with foreign powers, allusions have been made to their domestic disturbances or foreign wars, to their revolutions or dissensions. It may be proper to observe that this is done solely in cases where those events affect our political relations with them or to show their operation on our commerce. Further than this, it is neither our policy nor our right to interfere.
>
> Our best wishes on all occasions, our good offices when required, will be afforded, to promote the domestic tranquility and foreign peace of all nations with whom we have any intercourse. Any intervention in their affairs further than this, even by the expression of an official opinion, is contrary to our principles of international policy, and will always be avoided.[6]

Despite these words, it is often pointed out that the United States did indeed protest against the treatment of Jews in Syria, Persia, Rumania, Serbia, the Ottoman Empire and most notably Russia during the latter half of the nineteenth century. Yet, these are more appropriately viewed as isolated instance of intercession which serve rather to confirm America's overall unwillingness to become involved in the domestic matters of other states. In 1858, for example, President Buchanan refused to intercede in the case of the six year old secretly baptised child of Jewish parents abducted by Papal guards in Bologna. American envoys in different countries often disagreed on the appropriateness or effectiveness of humanitarian intercession. When American envoys did take a stance on such matters, they took great pains to assure officials that they had no intention of urging changes in the domestic laws or "to make any imperative demand of a nature to embarrass."[7]

The options for humanitarian intercession were thus very narrowly defined. Blanket approval was given only in cases where U.S. citizens were prevented from exercising rights they customarily enjoyed at home. Beyond that, diplomacy was guided by respect for sovereignty and foreign domestic laws, even when those were not in accordance with our own domestic statutes. When concerted efforts were made to change a nation's policies, as in the case of Rumania's leniency against perpetrators of crimes against Jews, the United States acted either in conjunction with or subsequent to the involvement of other major powers. Thus, it could always argue that a diplomatic precedent had been set.

Humanitarian intercession was further restricted to instances where it was deemed effective in preventing further violence, or to redress the grievances of specific individuals. If other nations had attempted such intercession and been rebuffed, or if discussions with the government proved fruitless or counterproductive, the United States would rarely pursue the issue further. Vague admonitions on the domestic conduct of foreign countries were eschewed.

During the last two decades of the nineteenth and then on into this century, the plight of Russian Jews aroused increasing concern in this country. Yet, the most significant action taken with regard to their status, the abrogation in 1911 of the Treaty of Navigation and Commerce between the two nations, again concerned the rights of American (Jewish) citizens who had been denied visas to visit Russia and was taken against the wishes of President Taft and Secretary of State Knox.[8]

During the nation's first century and a bit beyond, therefore, our efforts at humanitarian diplomacy were clearly circumscribed by the limitations of our power. As our abilities to shape world events grew, however, so did the desire of many to match this influence with a new and broader definition of the purposes of American diplomacy. The first President to do so unequivocally was Woodrow Wilson.

Deeply religious and a fervent believer that it was America's mission to enhance democracy not only at home but abroad, Wilson felt that democracy was the ultimate expression of the goals and interests of humanity. He expected it to spread with relative ease to every country and, unlike his predecessors drew no distinctions between international and national obligations.[9] For example, Wilson felt it was improper to recognize regimes that did not conform to America's moral and constitutional standards. He therefore forged a new definition of legitimacy and the recognition of states which made constitutional government, rather than the *de facto* existence of a government, the determining factor. On these grounds he refused recognition to the regime of Victoriano Huertain in 1913 ("a mere military despotism").

Wilson's "new diplomacy launched," in Latin America, found its intended culmination in the League of Nations, Wilson's vehicle for a world order of peace and benevolence. Upon his arrival in Paris, Wilson stated his objectives thus:

> Why has Jesus Christ so far not succeeded in inducing the world to follow his teachings in these matters? It is because he taught the ideal without devising any practical means of attaining it. That is why I am proposing a practical scheme to carry out this aim.[10]

Wilson's fervor for his Fourteen Point peace plan caused French delegate George Clemenceau to quip, "God had ten commandments but Wilson has fourteen."

Wilson was perhaps the first President for whom American foreign policy culminated in the Americanization of the rest of the globe. The League was America's chance to "redeem her pledges to the world," and to show that through her guidance humanity could be pulled out of its age-long misery.[11] An irate Senate, angry at having been slighted by Wilson and still leery of foreign entanglements, temporarily eclipsed Wilson's ideological influence, but there was little hope of returning to isolation now that the nation was firmly established as a world power.

By 1940, President Roosevelt perceived the need to anchor self-determination (Wilson's predominant concern) more firmly among other acknowledged rights. He confided to Willard Range his feeling that the nation would never be wholly safe at home until all other nations recognized and implemented such freedoms as were guaranteed in the United States.[12] The next year, in his "Four Freedoms" address to Congress, Roosevelt revised the traditional presumption of complete national sovereignty in favor of principle that would allow Great Power (later United Nations) intervention to correct egregious human rights violations. For the first time the security of the United States was directly linked to internal conditions in foreign nations, and human rights gained a lasting foothold in international politics.

When President Truman espoused the containment of communism, the humanitarian aspect of this policy was prominently displayed. Since Truman, Presidents and Secretaries of State of both parties have been united in condemning Soviet-style communism. In their minds, human rights and self-determination became synonymous with anti-communism. But the escalation of the Cold War soon caused anti-communism to far outdistance our human rights concerns in visibility and influence, eventually leaving them so far behind that contemporary observers have had difficulty discerning any clearly humanitarian component to our post-war containment policy. Later critics have taken containment and anti-communism to task for our ill-conceived involvement in Southeast Asia, and blamed it for engendering the amoralism in our foreign policy and lack of concern for the rights of individuals in non-communist nations.

Anti-communism and containment, however, were not lacking in a humanitarian idealism; rather, they may be viewed as a natural extension of attempts begun decades earlier to join humanitarian concern for the welfare of other peoples with perceived threats to our national security. By the 1960s, the era of America's most extensive peacetime involvement in world affairs, policy rationale was commonly couched in terms that drew no distinction between humanitarian concerns and national security objectives. To obviate criticism the two were conflated, blurring any constraints on American involvement in terms of either scope or objectives. The contradictory solutions to our overextension offered during the 1970s demonstrate how much the two are interwoven in today's policy debates. While some called for a sharp curtailment of American involvement abroad, many of the same people argued that human rights should be made "the heart of our foreign policy," a course which would hardly diminish our global involvement. We had arrived at a qualitatively different understanding of the American mission than that which the Founding Fathers held.

III

The power that the United States has to influence world events constitutes a great temptation to exert such influence to remold the world in our image. As a result we have tended to confuse two applications of that power which perhaps are best kept separate or at least must be distinguished: the exercise of power in our national security interests, and the exercise of power for humanitarian concerns that do not reflect our national security concerns narrowly defined. Attempting to distinguish these two broad purposes, both of which have strong domestic support, especially in the application of America's power in the world could be one step toward implementing what philosophers and statesmen through our history have called practical morality.

NOTES

1. Paul A. Varg, *Foreign Policies of the Founding Fathers* (East Lansing: Michigan State University, 1963), 3.

2. Felix Gilbert, *To the Farewell Address* (Princeton: Princeton University, 1961), 86.

3. William Spence Robinson, "The Recognition of the Hispanic Nations by the United States," *Hispanic American Historical Review*, 1, # 3 (August 1918), 253.

4. Edward M. Earle, "American Interest in the Greek Cause," *American Historical Review*, 33, # 1 (October 1927), 49.

5. John C. Rives, *Appendix to the Congressional Globe* 32nd Congress, 1st Session 35 (Washington, D.C., 1852), 309.

6. Rives, *Congressional Globe*, 181.

7. Cyrus Adler and David Margolith, *With Firmness in the Right* (Salem: Ayer Company, 1946), 311-2.

8. Peter G. Filene, *Americans and the Soviet Experiment* (Cambridge: Harvard University, 1967), 11.

9. "When properly directed, there is no people not fitted for self-government," Wilson confidently averred. Quoted in Frank J. Merli and Theodore A. Wilson, *Makers of American Diplomacy* (New York: Scribner's, 1974), 61.

10. Quoted in John G. Stoessinger, *Crusaders and Pragmatists* (New York: Norton, 1979), 21.

11. Gordon N. Levin, *Woodrow Wilson and World Politics* (New York: Oxford University, 1968), 256.

12. M. Glenn Johnson, "Historical Perspectives on Human Rights and U.S Foreign Policy" *Universal Human Rights*, 2 (July-September 1980), 13.

PART THREE

The Nuclear Crisis

Missile Defense and
Political Language
Robert A. Strong

In March of 1983 Ronald Reagan delivered his surprising speech about ballistic missile defense, and ever since, there has been public confusion about what to call the programs and policies that the president's speech set in motion. Initially they were dubbed "Star Wars" by journalists who wished to convey the dramatic nature of the president's proposal and the fact that the kind of missile defense he alluded to would be likely to involve elaborate space-based weapons capable of shooting down Soviet missiles in, what was then called, the "high frontier." Almost as soon as the term Star Wars began to make headlines, the administration insisted that it be replaced by Strategic Defense Initiative or SDI. For the most part, the media has cooperated with the administration of the Great Communicator, and now regularly uses Strategic Defense Initiative and SDI, with parenthetical explanations that the administration's missile defense program is popularly known as star wars. Critics of SDI or star wars, whether they use the official or the popular nomenclature, often attack the President for his plans to build anti-ballistic missile systems which will violate the 1972 ABM treaty. It is likely that citizens will have some difficulty understanding how something called SDI could pose a threat to an ABM agreement, or why either of these acronyms would be of any concern to Obi-Wan-Kenobi.

When important political issues are debated in confusing terminology, there is a danger that vital policy decisions will be made before the public fully understands what is at stake. With regard to ballistic missile defenses, we are living in just such a dangerous period; and unless we speak clearly about the questions that are before us, we run a real risk of giving the wrong answers or, what is worse, having no answers at all.

The administration's Strategic Defense Initiative consists of two reasonably distinct endeavors. One is research into new technologies that would operate in space, or use space-based elements, to destroy Soviet missiles as early as possible in their brief flight to the United States. These technologies may involve advanced lasers, enormous mirrors in earth orbit, particle beams, or the x-rays generated by nuclear explosions. There is absolutely nothing wrong with calling such a program star wars. If the phrase brings to mind an image of Luke Skywalker sitting in the ultimate swivel chair firing beams of light at multitudes of enemies with the help of his ever reliable computer companion, it may not be misleading. Successfully shooting down all of the Soviet missiles or warheads that could be aimed at the United States would probably require the development of some, as yet unavailable, reliable and efficient destructive beam of energy. It would also demand the near perfect coordination of target identification, tracking, and homing currently available only in motion pictures and video games, not to mention the use of computers with abilities resembling some combination of R2D2's analytical skills and C3PO's mastery of communications. This is not to say that space-based missile defense using new technologies is forever impossible, or not worth thinking about. We have been doing this sort of research for decades, as have the Soviets. Research will no doubt continue, but the products that will emerge from it, probably belong to a distant future, if not to a distant galaxy; and efforts to develop immature systems on a crash basis are apt to be both futile and enormously expensive. Calling the space-based research of SDI "Star Wars" may convey exactly the right message and raise precisely the right questions about how and when we could provide for this kind of defense.

The other half of the Strategic Defense Initiative involves the possibility of using existing equipment and know-how to build missile defenses in space, or on the ground, within the very near future; and here a different language problem emerges. There is already a phrase and an acronym for such programs. They are called anti-ballistic missile systems or ABMs. Like IRS or KGB, ABM is an acronym with a distinct political history. There was a long and bitter debate in the late 1960s and early 1970s about the wisdom of building ABMs; and because they were both costly and ineffective, they received congressional support only as a bargaining chip for the SALT I negotiations. Unlike most bargaining chips this one was actually traded in, and in 1972 the United States and the Soviet Union agreed that neither side would ever build more than a negligible number of stationary ground-based ABMs. The ABM treaty also provided that neither party would "develop, test, or deploy ABM systems or components which are sea-based, air-based, space-based, or mobile land-based."[1] The treaty contained other provisions, including those that are the focus of current technical disputes about the legality of new and upgraded multi-purpose radar installations, but the essence of the treaty was a practical prohibition of ABMs — both the types of ABMs that existed in the 1960s and all the other types that were then imagined. And the essence of the treaty has been observed by both sides. If this administration is preparing to violate the 1972 treaty by developing, testing, or deploying a new generation of ABM defenses, it should be honest and say so. The Russians are not likely to be fooled by an ABM program that is called a Strategic Defense Initiative, even if some Americans are.

The research into a future Star Wars defense, or the deployment of an ABM defense, or the construction of a layered defense, involving both old and new technologies put in place over a long period of time, would be a very expensive undertaking. It would encourage Soviet programs to match and counter American efforts. At its best, such a program offers little hope of making nuclear weapons "impotent and obsolete," as President Reagan promised in 1983. But moving beyond pure research into missile defense technologies will definitely render the ABM Treaty both impotent and obsolete. Choosing to do so may arguably be in the interest of the United States, even if missile defenses in the 1980s, like those in the 1960s, are costly and imperfect. But the abrogation of the most important arms control agreement of the postwar era is a major decision with long-term implications for East-West relations and for the future of the superpower arms competition. It should not be taken lightly. It should not be disguised with confusing language. The terminology of SDI and the ambiguity about exactly what kinds of activities it involves, tends to postpone public debate about the future of the ABM Treaty. If debate is postponed long enough, the administration's missile defense programs will be well underway and will have gained all the momentum that usually accompany major military procurements. At that point debate may be too late.

"In our time," George Orwell once wrote, "political speech and writing are largely the defense of the indefensible....Thus political language has to consist largely of euphemism, question-begging and sheer cloudy vagueness."[2] SDI is a euphemism that begs innumerable questions and clouds important issues. If it is used at all, it should be clearly identified as the administration's preferred language. And in public discourse, it should be replaced by references to Star Wars research, or ABM deployments, or some other combination of words and letters that accurately describe the magnitude and the potential illegality of what the Reagan administation has proposed.

NOTES

1. Article V, Section 1. of the Treaty Between the United States of America and the Union of Soviet Socialist Republics on the Limitation of Anti-Ballistic Missile Systems.

2. The quote is from George Orwell "Politics and the English Language," in *The Collected Essays, Journalism and Letters of George Orwell*, Vol. 4, edited by Sonia Orwell and Ian Angus, (New York: Harcourt Brace Javanovich, 1968), p. 136.

PART FOUR

The Credibility of Leadership in the Future

Adlai Stevenson:
A Model for Future Leadership
by Don Mitchell

> I am in politics as a result of a personal decision to do what I
> could to help in building a peaceful world. That decision
> carried with it an obligation — the obligation to talk sense,
> to tell the truth as I see it, to discuss the realities of our
> situation, never to minimize the tasks that lie ahead. I don't
> know whether that is the way to win in politics, but it is the
> only way I want to win.[1]

In this dangerous nuclear age, the need for wise and responsible leadership is particularly compelling. It is, however, unrealistic and unreasonable to think that all who govern us will be endowed with the characteristics of a strong leader. We must attempt to define what characteristics constitute leadership and examine the likelihood of finding individuals with these necessary traits.

Many Americans complain about the lack of strong leadership in our country. In particular, Americans have increasingly taken to complaining about the poor choices we have for President. It is increasingly argued that the qualities that a candidate needs to win high office — ruthless ambition, wealth, organization, and skill in front of a television camera — do not necessarily make a good leader. What qualities should the American public look for in our leaders in this dangerous age?

Adlai Stevenson, who was born in 1900 and died in 1965, was an unsuccessful candidate for the office of President, yet he retained his role as an effective and articulate leader of the party in exile after his defeat at the polls. Would Adlai Stevenson have lived up to his enormous potential for leadership if he had won the Presidency? This is one of history's unanswerable questions. No one can say for sure. Every vote is an act of faith. But it can reasonably be argued that in his limited, but by no means insignificant capacity as leader of the opposition, Adlai Stevenson set a standard for responsible leadership that is worthy of emulation. Stevenson's leadership attributes deserve to be examined as a model for future leaders.

STEVENSON'S LEADERSHIP QUALITIES

Adlai Stevenson exerted considerable influence on his times as the Democratic candidate for the Presidency in 1952 and 1956. His eloquent and responsible leadership of the opposition during America's apogee of power in the 1950s made Adlai Stevenson a figure of national and international stature. The difficulty in assessing Stevenson's leadership is the fact that, except for one term as Governor of Illinois, he never held an elected office that would confer on him the necessary power that gives leadership its substance.

To understand Stevenson's views on responsible leadership, it is important to examine Stevenson's background and his views on the importance of the individual's role in a democracy. His own interest in pursuing a career in public office came as a result of his ancestors' role in public affairs. Stevenson was born into a political family that had played a notable role in American history. His maternal great-grandfather was Jesse Fell, a founder of the Republican Party, and a close friend and advisor to Abraham Lincoln. Adlai E. Stevenson, his paternal grandfather and namesake, was elected Grover Cleveland's Vice-President in 1892. Stevenson's father Lewis served as Secretary of State in Illinois and was active in national Democratic affairs for many years. Stevenson served as a lawyer in several of the New Deal agencies set up by the Roosevelt Administration. His strong advocacy of internationalism at the Chicago Council on Foreign Relations led to his involvement in the Committee to Defend America by Aiding the Allies prior to America's entry into World War II.

Stevenson's dedication to the importance of America's role in the world order and his determination to seek a career in public service was further strengthened by his work as special assistant to Secretary of the Navy Frank Knox during World War II. His participation in the war not only buttressed Stevenson's internationalism, but also served to reinforce his determination to seek a career in public service:

> Somewhere, there in Italy, I think, I read about a public-opinion poll which reported that some seven out of ten American parents disapproved of their sons going into politics or public service, or something like that. From what I had already seen of the war at home, in the Pacific, in the Mediterranean and from what I was still to see in Europe, I've often thought of that little morsel of news; fight, suffer, die, squander our subsistence, yes; but work in peacetime for the things we die for in war, no! Small wonder, I thought,

that our "politics" is no better, and great wonder that it is as good as it is. It seems to me sad that "politics" and "politician" are so often epithets and words of disrespect and contempt, and not without justification, in the land of Jefferson and in a government by the governed.[2]

Stevenson's internationalism found meaningful expression in his service as a U.S. delegate to the Preparatory Commission of the United Nations where he played a significant role in setting up the fledgling organization. After his World War II experience, Stevenson went on to win an upset gubernatorial victory in Illinois in 1948. Stevenson's progressive administration as Governor of Illinois and his national appeal to fellow Democrats led him to be drafted as his party's candidate in 1952 against Dwight Eisenhower. After another defeat in 1956, he would go on to serve as the United States' Permanent Representative to the United Nations from 1961 until his death in 1965.

Adlai Stevenson was an anomaly — a politician who disdained the artificial aspects of politics and sought to appeal to the reason and not the emotions of the electorate. Stevenson had an abiding faith in the application of reason and intelligence to the problems of society. He constantly stressed that while the American people had rights, they had responsibilities as well. John Kennedy's inaugural call to "ask not what your country can do for you, ask what you can do for your country" was nothing more than an amplification of the Stevenson credo. Stevenson never stopped calling on Americans to participate in their nation's affairs. As Stevenson admonished a group of Princeton students in 1954:

You know that our record as citizens in recent years has been something less than perfect. Too often our citizens have ignored their duty to their government. Too often they have not even bothered to vote. But this is not all. Participating in government in a democracy does not mean merely casting a ballot on election day. It means much more than that. It means an attitude, a moral view, and a willingness to assume day-to-day responsibility.[3]

He believed that it was vital for individuals to not only be informed and concerned about government, but they must be actively involved in the system as well.

Stevenson lived what he preached — an informed and responsible citizen who became involved in the public affairs of his times. He passionately believed that it was the duty of each citizen to become involved in the political process. His intelligence, eloquence, and wit inspired a new generation of Americans to become involved in the political process. He believed that government can only be as effective and responsible as the citizenry permits: "Your public servants serve you right; indeed often they serve you better than your apathy and indifference deserve."[4]

To Stevenson, it was essential for a leader to appeal to the reason, and not merely the emotions, of the people. He was repulsed by the tendency of candidates and leaders to appeal to the perceived lowest common denominator of public interest, over-simplifying complex issues, and offering easy, painless options. As Stevenson wrote to his friend Archibald MacLeish during the 1952 Presidential campaign:

> I get so sick of the everlasting appeals to the cupidity and prejudices of every group which characterizes our political campaigns. There is something finer in people; they know that they *owe* something too. I should like to try, at least to appeal to their sense of obligation as well as their avarice.[5]

The best example of Stevenson's firm belief in the need to appeal to the reason of the electorate was his approach to foreign policy during the Cold War years. To Stevenson, just as important as what America did in the international arena was how America went about enunciating and formulating its foreign policy objectives. Policy-makers must be responsible, not only in their actions, but in the rhetoric they use to articulate foreign policy. The general tendency of policy-makers to proclaim the need to "get tough" with the communists, and tailor general foreign policy objectives to the vagaries of public opinion, particularly in an election year, was, and continues to be, an unfortunate byproduct of the American political system. This tendency is pervasive in our time and was particularly strong in the Eisenhower years, with the rabid anti-communism exploited by Senator Joseph McCarthy and the self-righteousness of Secretary of State John Foster Dulles.

The bombastic rhetoric of the Eisenhower Administration did not frighten the communists nearly as much as it frightened American allies, who feared that they could be the first victims of nuclear retaliation. If anything, such talk was creating a decline in confidence toward the United States.

While ever an idealist, Stevenson was essentially a realist in his approach to American foreign policy during the Cold War. He believed that America would best serve its national interests only when it realized the limits of its power and influence in the world. In the dangerous atomic age, the United States must learn to see its long-term interests in the collective and work toward a cooperative, cohesive world order which promotes freedom and justice, and avoids the cataclysmic dangers of modern war that could be precipitated by reckless rhetoric and actions.

The real question is not who can stand up or talk back to the Russians. That's too easy. The real question is who can sit down with them at the bargaining table and negotiate with them from a position of strength and confidence. The real question is not who is tough and who is soft. The real question is who is wise and who is foolish, who likes to play with words and who likes to get things done.[6]

Attendant to Stevenson's belief in the importance of appealing to the reason of the citizenry was his belief that a leader must be willing to tell hard truths and face unpleasant realities. In his 1952 speech accepting his party's nomination, the only genuine draft in the history of American politics, Stevenson said:

The ordeal of the twentieth century — the bloodiest, most turbulent era of the Christian age — is far from over. Sacrifice, patience, understanding and implacable purpose may be our lot for years to come. Let's face it. Let's talk sense to the American people. Let's tell them the truth, that there are no gains without pains, that we are now on the eve of great decisions, not easy decisions, like resistance when you're attacked, but a long, patient, costly struggle which alone can assure triumph over the great enemies of man — war, poverty and tyranny — and the assaults upon human dignity which are the most grievous consequences of each. ...Better we lose the election than mislead the people and better we lose than misgovern the people.[7]

This firm belief that a leader must tell hard, unpleasant truths, touches the core of true leadership — moral courage. By this is meant the courage to speak out in favor of a prudent course of policy when political expediency councils otherwise.

Stevenson was widely considered indecisive, but this indecision was reflected almost exclusively in his reluctance to push himself forward for public office. On matters of principle, Stevenson was unshakable, even when the costs were likely to be high and predictable. Many of the stands Stevenson took on public issues were highly unpopular and required great courage. His internationalism prior to World War II, his opposition to McCarthyism after World War II, his advocacy of a nuclear test ban, and his lonely position during the Cuban Missile Crisis calling for a negotiated settlement on outstanding issues with the Soviet Union, are only a few examples of Stevenson's adherence to principle over political expediency. His advocacy of nuclear disarmament and the need to deal with the problems posed by the underdeveloped Third World made him one of the most progressive and far-sighted figures of his time.

The tragedy of Stevenson's life was the fact that he never attained the necessary power to exercise true leadership. Stevenson subordinated his pursuit of power to transcendent intellectual and moral values. As Hans Morgenthau said of Stevenson after his death in 1965, "He wanted power, but he wanted it only with intellectual and moral reservations openly revealed."[8] Stevenson pursued power, but in a seemingly half-hearted, complicated fashion. Stevenson's characteristics — his thoughtful, candid, ruminative approach to complex issues, his honestly expressed self-doubts, his eloquence and wit — which made him such an appealing individual, were too dominant in his personality for the good of his political ambitions. His leadership qualities, while rare among public figures, raised doubts in an electorate that often seems to prefer its national leaders to project a confident image of strong leadership without regard to whether or not they possess the responsible substance of leadership.

The American electorate likes its candidates for office to be uncomplicated and straightforward in their pursuit of power. Americans are skeptical of candidates who do not stress their ordinariness during a campaign. Stevenson's principled yet ambivalent quest for power won the admiration but not the confidence of the electorate. Unfortunately, it seems that ordinariness, not greatness, is most likely to gain power in our system of government.

PROSPECTS FOR THE FUTURE

When Stevenson accepted his Party's nomination, he had no real campaign organization, no campaign funds, no position papers, and no campaign strategy. The election was three months and nine days away. Needless to say, Stevenson lost overwhelmingly to Dwight Eisenhower, the friendly, grandfatherly hero figure. After twenty years of tumultuous Democratic rule that witnessed the elevation of the United States to a world power and transformed the face of American government, Americans were clearly in the mood for a caretaker Administration that asked for little in the way of sacrifice.

Americans seem to be in the same mood today. Even with unprecedented budget and trade deficits and a dangerously spiraling arms race, Ronald Reagan's personal popularity is unassailable. A frustrated Stevenson remarked on this same phenomenon when he ran against Eisenhower: "Never did anyone make such a success of being a cheerleader — never in his career has he been identified with an un-popular decision." During the 1956 election, farmers were dissatisfied with Administration farm policy but many were still going to vote for the likable Ike, the first teflon-coated President of modern times. Stevenson would tell the story about asking a farmer who was unhappy about the Eisenhower farm policy why people weren't mad at Ike. The farmer replied, "Oh, no one connects *him* with the Administration."[9]

Stevenson acknowledged that "history is not noted for being kind to the losers." Indeed, history does tend to be more charitable toward the winners. Dwight Eisenhower's presidency has undergone a major reassessment by many revisionist historians. He was, they argue, a "hidden hand President" who kept a low profile but was a shrewd, in-telligent, pragmatist who operated effectively behind the scenes. While he was certainly not the genius that some revisionists suggest, there is merit to this revisionist interpretation of the Eisenhower Presidency. What is considered the conventional wisdom about a President during his term of office is often rejected by historians. Truman was considered an ineffective President, but history has depicted him as tough and decisive. Eisenhower was viewed as a lethargic and detached leader. History has depicted him otherwise. It is now the conventional wisdom that Ronald Reagan is a Great Communicator, consistently underestimated, and one of the best leaders of his time. One cannot help but wonder how history will depict him.

It's difficult not to long for a return to Stevensonian appeals to the electorate's intelligence, particularly after the 1984 national campaign that witnessed such rhetorical heights as "Where's the beef?" and "You ain't seen nothin' yet!" Ronald Reagan receives a great deal of praise for being a Great Communicator and he is widely regarded as the most effec-tive communicator since John Kennedy. Actually, this is more a reflec-tion of the dearth of likable, politically adept men who have occupied the White House since Kennedy's time than on Mr. Reagan's rhetorical talents. By any objective criteria, it is difficult not to be appalled by the inaninities and inaccuracies he utters during press conferences. But a timid political opposition seems too cowed by the President's popularity to take him effectively to task.

Reagan reduces vitally important, complex issues to simple images of good and bad, American and un-American.[10] Like Willy Loman, salesman Reagan is "way out there in the blue, riding on a smile and a shoeshine." As a frustrated Stevenson said of the appeal of the bland but reassuring Ike, "I think we realize that mediocrity, materialism, social indifference and repulsive showmanship cannot be forever disguised by wholesome smiles, golf clubs, and a Bible firmly clutched beneath the right arm — if seldom read."[11]

As previously discussed, another word for honesty is leadership. The failure of this kind of leadership among our elected officials is why our current budget is an unprecedented disaster. Most of the blame for this situation belongs to Ronald Reagan. He's the one with charisma and a political mandate, yet he refuses to confront the difficult choices that must be made to safeguard our future prosperity. His reputation is based on leadership which consists of telling people what they want to hear.[12] True leadership is persuading people to accept important truths that they don't want to hear. Leadership was Harry Truman persuading Americans of the need to finance the Marshall Plan, Lyndon Johnson gaining passage for the Civil Rights Act, Richard Nixon normalizing relations with the People's Republic of China, and Jimmy Carter obtaining ratification of the Panama Canal Treaties in the face of stiff opposition. Leadership isn't persuading people to take a tax cut. Adlai Stevenson understood this better than most:

> The true function of a political leader in a democracy is not to impose his will upon the people but to aid them in making proper choices. Harder than charting the course of public policy, harder even than converting generalities into details, is the indispensable task of explanation; indispensable because the political leader only proposes but the people dispose. He must explain and try to lead them to the truth.[13]

In our quest for better and wiser government, we should, as historian Barbara Tuchman suggests,[14] first apply the test of character to our prospective leaders. At the heart of any test of character is the distinguishing attribute of moral courage. It is too much to expect our leaders to have additional attributes of genius and eloquence. So few individuals possess these characteristics in the world today, let alone in the field of public affairs. But the attributes of candor, decency, moderation, and courage are within the grasp of each individual. Unfortunately, our political system is structured to reward well-financed organization and ruthless ambition instead of these qualities.

The structure of America's political system makes it unlikely that a leader with Adlai Stevenson's characteristics will appear in the future. The circumstances in 1952 that brought about Stevenson's meteoric appearance on the national political scene are highly unlikely to be repeated. John Kennedy's successful quest for the Presidency in 1960 ushered in a new age of political Darwinism — the era of the engineer politician.

Our electoral process is currently dominated by commercial techniques of fund-raising and image-making at the expense of an examination of leadership qualities in our officials. The quest for power in our system eclipses the prospects for better government performance. Increasingly, a guiding principle of our leaders is to please the majority while offending as few voters as possible. Consequently, the quality of our national Presidential campaigns has diminished over the last several decades.

The most realistic goal of our society must be not to attempt to educate potential leaders so much as to educate the electorate to recognize integrity of character and reject the artificial. Perhaps it is unrealistic to expect any better leadership than mankind has experienced in the last several thousand years. But in this age of nuclear anxiety, we can no longer afford mediocrity in our leaders. The dangers are far too great.

NOTES

1. Adlai E. Stevenson, *The New America* (New York: Harper & Brothers, 1957), pp. 33-34.
2. John Bartlow Martin, *Adlai Stevenson of Illinois* (Garden City: Doubleday & Company, Inc., 1976), p. 217.
3. Walter Johnson (ed.), *The Papers of Adlai E. Stevenson, Volume IV: "Let's Talk Sense to the American People," 1952-1955* (Boston: Little, Brown and Company, 1974), p. 340.
4. Adlai E. Stevenson, *Major Campaign Speeches of Adlai E. Stevenson: 1952* (New York: Random House, 1953), p. 101.
5. Walter Johnson (ed.), *The Papers of Adlai E. Stevenson, Volume IV: "Let's Talk Sense to the American People," 1952-1955* (Boston: Little, Brown and Company, 1974), p. 39.
6. John Bartlow Martin, *Adlai Stevenson and the World* (Garden City: Doubleday & Company, Inc., 1977), p. 543.
7. Walter Johnson (ed.), *The Papers of Adlai E. Stevenson, Volume IV: "Let's Talk Sense to the American People," 1952-1955* (Boston: Little, Brown and Company, 1974), pp. 18-19.
8. Hans J. Morgenthau, "Stevenson — Tragedy and Greatness," *The New Republic* (7 August 1965), p. 19.
9. John Bartlow Martin, *Adlai Stevenson and the World* (Garden City: Doubleday & Company, Inc., 1977), p. 345.
10. Leslie H. Gelb, "The Mind of the President," *The New York Times Magazine* (6 October 1985), p. 113.
11. John Bartlow Martin, *Adlai Stevenson and the World* (Garden City: Doubleday & Company, Inc., 1977), p. 193.
12. "Honesty and Happy Talk," *The New Republic* (5 August 1985), p. 7.

13. Walter Johnson (ed.), *The Papers of Adlai E. Stevenson, Volume III: Governor of Illinois, 1949-1953* (Boston: Little, Brown and Company, 1973), p. 516.
14. Barbara W. Tuchman, *The March of Folly: From Troy to Vietnam* (New York: Alfred A. Knopf, 1984), pp. 386-387.

Theological and Ethical Reflection in Service of the Future

William H. Boley

PRELIMINARY CONSIDERATIONS

Since there are those who might wonder about how theological and ethical reflection can be of service[1] to institutions and leaders as they envision and strive to realize their vision of the future, I should offer some preliminary justification for the enterprise undertaken in this essay. The importance of theological and ethical reflection for ecclesiastical institutions and leaders should be clear enough. Precisely how theological and ethical reflection can be of service to social institutions and leaders may be less apparent. In this regard, at least two broad considerations should be noted. First, theological and ethical language has been and continues to be used frequently in public discourse, and, thus, should be subject to careful scrutiny. It seems only fair that if those who carry on this discourse are determined to make forays into the theological and ethical realm, they should take no offense if theologians and ethicians think themselves justified in offering comment and criticism about their use of this language. A second reason for reflecting theologically and ethically on the shape of institutions is the light such reflection can shed on efforts to envision and to strive to build these institutions. This is the case in that such reflection can serve to enlarge our vision and provide impetus for our strivings, while reminding us of the provisional character of both our vision and our strivings.

I do not doubt that these broad considerations will be unconvincing to those who are not already disposed by their own conviction or experience to believe in the importance of theological and ethical reflection for the efforts of institutions and leaders outside the ecclesiastical context. In a sense, the importance of theological and ethical reflection in this regard is to be measured by its fruitfulness. With this in mind, then, I turn now to an examination and evaluation of one strand of theological and ethical thought which has been extremely fruitful in shaping many of the leaders and the institutions of our time — the thought of Reinhold Niebuhr.

THE QUESTION POSED

In his day, Reinhold Niebuhr attempted to shore up the ark of Christian theological and ethical reflection against both its liberal inhabitants, who had allowed it to fall into disrepair, and the surging tides of the time, which threatened to swamp it. In our day, Niebuhr's Christian realism, while respected, is regarded by many as irrelevant, if not opposed to the concerns of the contemporary context. It is argued that if Protestant Liberalism was in the past a theological rationalization of bourgeois American culture because of its optimism, then in the present Niebuhr's Neorthodoxy provides through its pessimism an even more effective defense of that same culture.[2] Is Niebuhr's outlook nothing more than a venerable relic to be placed in the museum of Christian classics? Or does it provide a vessel of thought in which to navigate the problematic waters of the present, and perhaps even venture into the future? More specifically, how can it respond to the important challenge of the theologies of hope and of liberation?[3] It is this question on which our inquiry into the contemporary relevance of Niebuhr's thought will center.

PROVISIONAL ANSWERS

In a sense, all answers to the question about the continuing relevance of Niebuhr's outlook must be provisional, since our period, one of short seasons and fleeting fashions of thought, seems to allow no more than momentary assurance about even the most tried-and-true axioms. But perhaps an approach to an answer can be made if we first clear away some of the caricatures which often obscure the true contours of his thought.

A quick glance at the hectic pace of Niebuhr's life should be sufficient to allay fears that Christian realism leads necessarily to the apathy frequently attributed to it by its current critics. From his early years in a Detroit parish to his later years in academic life in New York, Niebuhr was always on the move, tirelessly teaching, writing, preaching, and wielding his prophetic influence in the sphere of national and international politics. Indeed, it was impossible for him "to remain aloof from the maelstrom, even though he early learned that the prospects of solving problems were modest at best." He was forever "impatient with the insufficiencies of every prevailing philosophy and system of thought" and with "society's stubborn resistance to change and its sanctifying of the status quo."[4] Even though failing health in later years restricted his formerly frantic schedule of work and required him to retire to his home in Massachusetts, he retained a passionate concern for the important intellectual and political events of the 1960s, and persisted in his restless quest to see actualized the impossible ideal of self-sacrificial love. Thus, there is no reason to doubt Niebuhr's own intentions: As he clearly stated in his late work, *Man's Nature and His Communities*, he wanted to place realism in the service of progressive justice.[5] In fact, all his writings, from the early articles on Henry Ford's pretended philanthropy to his last piercing Vietnam essays, convey his sincere wish to serve justice and seek love with his realism. "But if not for himself, his realism seems to have become a weapon in the hands of some of his followers who are afraid of radical social change."[6] We cannot though rightly render judgment on Niebuhr by observing the appropriation of his position by others, for even the most profound insights are subject to both proper use and misuse. Instead, we must scrutinize the content of his thought to discern if it is defensible in the present context.

Contrary to the repeated charges of his critics, Niebuhr's realism does not represent, nor does it encourage an inward, ahistorical theological outlook. Even though Niebuhr's anthropology and eschatology reflect the Neorthodox emphasis on transcendence and reconciliation, and so on inner, existential repentance and trust, it is still undeniable that his theology never became exclusively private or inward as much of Neorthodoxy did. Unlike Bultmann and Barth, Niebuhr uses Biblical, Reformation, and Existentialist insights to interpret social and communal, "objective" history, and to offer a framework and provide direction for political decision-making.[7] In fact, Niebuhr clearly shows his scorn for those Christian orthodoxies which are socially impotent. His polemic is captured succinctly in the following statement: "There is so little content in such a position that I would prefer to work with the superficial believers in utopia than ally myself with a kind of theological profundity which falsifies the immediate situation."[8]

This social bent in Niebuhr's thought is raised to the level of programmatic intention in the Gifford Lectures on human destiny, where he seeks a synthesis of Reformation insight and Renaissance wisdom. While remembering with the Reformation that all human achievements are corruptible, he nevertheless learns from the Renaissance "that life in history" always affords "new possibilities of the good and the obligation to realize them."[9] Thus, Niebuhr insists that, along with fidelity to biblical symbolism and the facts of social experience, one crucially important criterion for a body of theological and ethical thought is its ability to initiate creative political action for ever greater equality.[10] "As much as his present eschatological critics, therefore, his was a political and not a private, interiorized theology, a theology whose goal was creative *praxis*, not contemplative reflection."[11]

THE SHAPE OF NIEBUHR'S *PRAXIS*

Despite the clear conclusion that the goal of Niebuhr's theological outlook is creative *praxis* significant questions remain about its contemporary relevance: Why this sort of *praxis*? What should restrain humankind from aspiring toward an ideally imagined future, perhaps improving life though never attaining the vision? Where can the sounds of hope be heard in the writings in which Niebuhr articulates his thought? An adequate answer to these questions may be afforded by climbing three points of vantage which overlook and offer perspective on Niebuhr's position.

From the first we can clearly see that in Niebuhr's work there is a vision of the Kingdom of God which is the lure and judge of all human attitudes and actions. This vision serves negatively to preclude misdirected opportunism, easy accommodation to the status quo, and conscienceless compromise, and positively to provide impetus for imagining new goals and striving for their realization. Besides those passages in volume two of the *The Nature and Destiny of Man* which express his vision,[12] we might also recall *Moral Man and Immoral Society*, where Niebuhr quotes approvingly a line from Shelley's "Prometheus": "hope, till hope creates/from its own wreck the thing it contemplates."[13] In the same work, Niebuhr also makes the claim that the "truest visions of religion are illusions, which may be partially realized by being resolutely believed,"[14] and concludes by referring to the "valuable illusion" that "the collective life of mankind can achieve perfect justice." Niebuhr characteristically finds that illusion "dangerous because it encourages terrible fanaticisms," yet desirable because it drives humankind to higher approximations of justice.[15]

Admittedly, affirmations like these are difficult to locate in the Niebuhrian literature. One has to look closely to see them, partly because his interpreters point so often to the dark foreground of his portrait of history's corruptions, while overlooking the light on the horizon of his thought which represents the transcendent fulfillment of history. But perhaps a second, historical point of observation will serve to explain the predominance of dark realism in Niebuhr's outlook.

Niebuhr preached in a period when the surging tide of capitalism receded, leaving behind depression, and he taught in a time when totalitarianism stirred up genocide, global war, and the threat of nuclear destruction. In such an era, an accent on realism was appropriate, indeed, it would have been outrageous, if not obscene, to dream about man's possibilities when nightmares of his own making were a reality in Dachau and Nagasaki. Our assessment of Niebuhr, then, must be historically sensitive, and with this observation in mind, we climb to a third vantage point from which to survey his thought.

From this perspective, we see what is perhaps the most pivotal and important reason for Niebuhr's deemphasis of the motif of hope, what might be described as "a watershed in theological argument" between his position and that maintained by the exponents of a theology of hope and a theology of liberation.[16] What I mean by this can be seen by referring to Jurgen Moltmann's ground-breaking work, *Theology of Hope*. Moltmann's work proceeds by way of negative definition, that is, he surveys and critiques various contemporary approaches to doing theology before he proceeds to develop his own constructive claim that theology is eschatology. Now although Moltmann does not explicitly address Niebuhr's position in his work, undoubtedly Niebuhr would be classified along with Barth and Bultmann as a theologian of "transcendental eschatology."[17] This means that the fundamental dialectic in Niebuhr's outlook is not between present and future, a temporal dialectic, but between transcendence and creatureliness, between time and eternity, between God and world. Such a vertical dialectic indicates that the transcendent is above and beyond, yet related to and impinging on every past, present, and future.[18] A clear illustration of this motif can be found in Niebuhr's striking statement that perfect love "*hovers* as a possibility and yet impossibility *over* all human life."[19] Thus, although temporality and the future and openness to it play an important role in Niebuhr's theological perspective, they by no means establish its parameters. "It is the vertical dialectic that is in this sense definitive," providing the model by which all other categories are discussed and elaborated, from anthropology to Christology to eschatology.[20]

Perhaps what is meant here can be illuminated best by contrasting Niebuhr's anthropology with that of the theologians of hope and liberation.[21] For them, human nature is understood as human primarily in relation to the "not yet." It is defined by openness to the future and hope for it, as, likewise, human destiny is conceived as a life lived in commitment to and action toward what is to come. In contrast, for Niebuhr, openness to the future represents the essential or ontological situation of humanity, not its redemptive possibility.[22] In this situation, human beings face contingent possibilities in their creaturely aspect and infinite possibilities insofar as they are also "free spirit." This dual openness to the future creates the conditions for human problems as much as it points to the possibilities for perfection because out of it arises anxiety which becomes the occasion for "the fall." "Man sins not because he is bound to his past....He sins because he is *not* bound to his past, because he is open to the future and all of its possibilities, and so without faith and trust he is, as contingent, anxious *in* that openness and makes himself God, obscuring that contingency and finitude which were made unsupportable *by* that openness."[23] Thus, hope does not afford the answer to the dilemma of human nature and destiny for Niebuhr, but faith which makes the open future with all its myriad ambiguities bearable. Faith, then, must have primacy over hope. This outlook, I believe Niebuhr would argue,[24] is psychologically and phenomenologically more sound than the position taken by the eschatologists, especially so in an age where the future is shadowed by a cloud like the one that mushroomed over Hiroshima.[25] With this in mind, we must proceed to a more careful assessment of the situation in the world today and the appropriateness of Niebuhr's perspective to it.

BETWEEN SENTIMENTALITY AND DESPAIR

Recent decades have been characterized by rising expectation and determination among those long oppressed, that is, among those who are poor, black, female, or who live in the third world. In addition, the fire kindled in these crusades has been fueled by scientific and technological advances which hold out hope that age-old problems such as world hunger might be overcome. In a time such as this, it is important to ask if a realism like Niebuhr's would not deflate the hopeful drive of these forces, and so prove to be a self-fulfilling prophecy. Likewise, it is appropriate to wonder whether a future-orientation is not needed, both in order to prevent a narrow fixation on the sins of the past or the problems of the present and in order to provide the impetus to overcome them. In short, don't the theologies of hope and liberation properly discern the signs of these times, and so indicate the direction our *praxis* should pursue?

Niebuhr would probably respond to this challenge to his position with a characteristic "Yes, but..." *Yes*, it is appropriate to set our sights on future possibilities: because of the *agape* of the Kingdom of God, "there are no limits to be set in history for the achievement of more universal brotherhood, for the development of more perfect and more inclusive mutual relations."[26] *But* such progress is no "simple possibility." Heady hopes must be grounded in the sober realities of history: "Higher realizations of historic justice would be possible if it were more fully understood that all such realizations contain contradictions to, as well as approximations of, the ideal of love. Sanctification in the realm of societal relations demands recognition of the impossibility of perfect sanctification."[27]

In this sense, then, Niebuhr's realism can be seen not as a brake on the achievements which might be brought about by hope, but as the only motor which will serve to power us toward hope's ends in the long haul of history. Only in this realistic way it might be argued is it possible to speak of sustaining hope and of steering a course toward its horizon between the Scylla and Charybdis of sentimentality and despair.[28] As John Bennet put it in an important symposium on this issue in *Christianity and Crisis*: "Nothing has happened to refute the realistic analysis of the stubbornness of evil in society or the tragic side of history. No return to a pre-Niebuhrian optimism is possible."[29] Not only is this impossible for Christian realists, but as recent events in Central and South America have indicated, it is equally impossible for those who buoy themselves with Christian hope. [30] Thus, while it seems that the eschatologists have discerned something of the real difficulties of our time, the hopelessness of the poor and the apathy of the rich, at the moment when they succeed in engaging people in action, especially political action, Niebuhr's voice will need to be heard again.[31]

THE TEMPTATION TO PRIDE AND THE PARADOX OF GRACE

Around the nucleus of Niebuhr's thought about hope and the possibilities of history revolves another sphere of interest which is appropriate to consider in our analysis of his contemporary relevance, that is, the temptation to pride and the paradox of grace. Those committed to the theologies of hope and liberation sometimes question the wisdom of talk about the pervasive reality of sin and the repeated need for confession. Such talk, it is claimed, might hobble efforts to change things by causing a retreat from the trenches of action. In response to this claim, though, Niebuhr is ready with the reminder that all who flex the muscles of power and who frequent the corridors of influence are assailed by great and grave temptations. No one is exempt from such temptations, neither the poor nor the religious. Thus, although he acknowledged their needs, Niebuhr was willing to allow only a provisional trust in the poor: "Every historic group has its own unique contribution to make. But there is no form of human goodness which cannot and will not be corrupted, particularly in the day of its success....Only the person who allows unconscious utopian illusions to be transmuted into conscious lies" will not concede "that a too unqualified trust in the poor man as redeemer will be the very force by which the poor man becomes untrustworthy."[32] Likewise, of one with well-known Christian commitments, Niebuhr wrote: "Cromwell really wanted to do the will of God — and thought he was doing it. Yet nothing in Cromwell's religion could save his dictatorship from being abortive and self-devouring."[33]

According to Niebuhr, then, it is clear that those who turn to moral and religious claims to justify their actions should be admonished about the temptations of power, and this especially since "the sad experiences of Christian history show how human pride and spiritual arrogance rise to new heights precisely at the point where the claims of sanctity are made."[34] In addition, against all such pretention, it is important to reassert the paradox of grace: The more aware persons, even religious persons, are of the persistence of their sin, the more hope there is that new possibilities of love and justice will be realized. This point is made perhaps nowhere more clearly than in *The Nature and Destiny of Man*:

> Redemption does not guarantee elimination of the sinful corruptions, which are in fact increased whenever the redeemed claim to be completely emancipated from them. But the taint of sin upon all historical achievements does not destroy the possibility of such achievements nor the obligation to realize truth and goodness in history. The fulfillments of meaning in history will be the more untainted in fact, if purity is not prematurely claimed for them. All historical activities stand under this paradox of grace.... We may have it; and yet we do not have it. And we will have it the more purely in fact if we know that we have it only in principle.[35]

In summarizing this section, we can see that the other side of Niebuhr's realistic outlook is openness to criticism, even self-criticism, and that this is always pertinent, particularly when, as in our time, the temptation to pride comes clothed in our highest hopes and aspirations for the realization of new possibilities of love and justice.

RETROSPECT AND PROSPECT

In conclusion, it seems that Niebuhr's Christian realism is relevant to the contemporary context. It remains an important voice among others in at least these ways: (1) in that it precludes easy accomodation to the present and provides impetus for imagining future possibilities for the realization of love and justice; (2) in that it offers an outlook which can sustain the drive toward these possibilities while avoiding the dangers of sentimentality and despair; (3) in that it contains a self-critical aspect important in steering clear of the shoals of pride. To say this, of course, is not to suggest that Niebuhr's outlook is without weaknesses.[36] Still, it seems that at least in these three ways, Niebuhr's Christian realism could perform an important service for institutions and leaders as they envision and strive to realize their vision of the future.

NOTES

1 My notion of theological and ethical reflection as "service" is informed by H. Richard Niebuhr, *Radical Monotheism and Western Culture*. (New York: Harper and Row, 1970), pp.93-99.

2 The inspiration for phrasing the issue this way comes from Langdon Gilkey, "Reinhold Niebuhr's Theology of History," in *The Legacy of Reinhold Niebuhr*, ed. Nathan A. Scott, Jr. (Chicago: University of Chicago Press, 1974), p.37.

3 I do not mean to suggest (much less to argue) that these are the only or even the most defensible options for Christian belief and practice today. My aim here is much more modest: to show that these two options, especially when viewed in relation to one another, could serve to illuminate certain crucial issues for institutions and leaders as they envision and strive to realize their vision of the future.

4 Kenneth Thompson, "Niebuhr as Thinker and Doer," in *The Legacy of Reinhold Niebuhr*, ed. Nathan A. Scott, Jr. (Chicago: University of Chicago Press, 1974), p.101.

5 Reinhold Niebuhr, *Man's Nature and His Communities*. (New York: Scribners, 1965), p.24

6 Ruurd Veldhuis, *Realism Versus Utopianism?* (Assen, The Netherlands: Van Gorcum, 1975), p.125.

7 Gilkey, p.37f.

8 This statement is an excerpt from the correspondence preceding the Oxford Conference of the World Council of Churches in 1937. It is referred to by Roger Shinn in his essay "Realism, Radicalism, and Eschatology in Reinhold Niebuhr," in *The Legacy of Reinhold Niebuhr*, ed. Nathan A. Scott, Jr. (Chicago: University of Chicago Press, 1974), p.95.

9 R. Niebuhr, *The Nature and Destiny of Man*, Volume II, (New York: Scribners, 1943), p.207.

10 R. Niebuhr, *An Interpretation of Christian Ethics*, (New York: Harper Brothers, 1935), pp.84-122.

11 Gilkey, p.38.

12 e.g. R. Niebuhr, *ND*, II, pp. 287-321.

13 R. Niebuhr, *Moral Man and Immoral Society*, (New York: Scribners, 1932), p.25.

14 R. Niebuhr, *MMIS*, p.81.

15 R. Niebuhr, *MMIS*, p.277.

16 Gilkey, p.49.

17 Jurgen Moltmann, *Theology of Hope*, (New York: Harper and Row, 1967), pp.50-68.

18 Gilkey, p.40.

19 R. Niebuhr, *Reinhold Niebuhr on Politics*, Davis and Good, eds. (New York: Scribners, 1960), p.138.

20 Gilkey, p.40.

21 Though I have not made direct reference to the literature of liberation theology, I hope that my generalized comments are accurate enough to highlight what I believe to be significant differences between this movement and Niebuhr's realistic outlook.

22 Gilkey, p.43.

23 Gilkey, p.44.

24 I say "I believe Niebuhr would argue" this because, as Gilkey notes on pp.47f., Niebuhr "never faced an eschatological optimism about perfection in the future based neither on man's developing reason nor on grace working on human freedom, but on God's future action alone."

25 Though see Dennis McCann, *Christian Realism and Liberation Theology*, (Maryknoll, N.Y.:Orbis, 1981), p.127, where it is suggested that the "psychological type" addressed by Niebuhr's anthropology may be more appropriate to the North American activist than the Latin American poor.

26 R. Niebuhr, *ND*, II, p.85.

27 R. Niebuhr, *ND*, II, p.246f.

28 R. Niebuhr, *The Children of Light and the Children of Darkness*, (New York: Scribners, 1944), p.189; see also McCann, p.239.

29 John Bennett, "Christian Realism: A Symposium," in *Christianity and Crisis*, Vol. XXXIII, No. 14, 1968, p.176.

30 McCann, p.211

31 This is the case especially since at present liberation theology lacks much of the ethical bridgework which might lead to principled political action. On this point, see McCann, pp.209ff.

32 R. Niebuhr, *Beyond Tragedy*, (New York: Scribners, 1937), pp.130f

33 R. Niebuhr, *Christianity and Power Politics*, (New York: Scribners, 1940), p.163f.

34 R. Niebuhr, *ND*, II, p.122.

35 R. Niebuhr, *ND*, II, pp.213,243.

36 For an incisive analysis of some of these weaknesses, see McCann, especially pp.53,103,121ff.,237.

REFERENCES

Bennett, John. "Christian Realism: A Symposium," in *Christianity and Crisis*, Vol. XXXIII, No. 14., 1968.

Gilkey, Langdon. "Reinhold Niebuhr's Theology of History," in *The Legacy of Reinhold Niebuhr*, ed. Nathan A. Scott, Jr., Chicago: University of Chicago Press, 1974.

McCann, Dennis. *Christian Realism and Liberation Theology*, Maryknoll, N.Y.: Orbis, 1981.

Moltmann, Jurgen. *Theology of Hope*, New York: Harper & Row, 1967.

Niebuhr, H. Richard. *Radical Monotheism and Western Culture*, New York: Harper & Row, 1970.

Niebuhr, Reinhold. *Moral Man and Immoral Society*, New York: Scribners, 1932.

_____ *An Interpretation of Christian Ethics*, New York: Harper Brothers, 1935.

_____ *Beyond Tragedy*, New York: Scribners, 1937.

_____ *Christianity and Power Politics*, New York: Scribners, 1940.

_____ *The Nature and Destiny of Man*, Volume I, New York: Scribners, 1941.

_____ *The Nature and Destiny of Man*, Volume I, New York: Scribners, 1943.

_____ *The Children of Light and the Children of Darkness*, New York: Scribners, 1944.

_____ *Love and Justice*, D.B. Robertson, ed., Philadelphia Westminister Press, 1957.

_____ *Reinhold Niebuhr on Politics*, Davis and Good, eds, New York: Scribners, 1960.

_____ *Man's Nature and His Communities*, New York: Scribners, 1965.

Shinn, Roger. "Realism, Radicalism, and Eschatology in Reinhold Niebuhr," in *The Legacy of Reinhold Niebuhr*, ed. Nathan A. Scott, Jr., Chicago: University of Chicago Press, 1974.

Thompson, Kenneth. "Niebuhr as Thinker and Doer," in *The Legacy of Reinhold Niebuhr*, ed. Nathan A. Scott, Jr., Chicago: University of Chicago Press, 1974.

Veldhuis, Ruurd. *Realism Versus Utopianism?*, Assen, The Netherlands: Van Gorcum: 1975.

Reading and Misreading Presidents

Robert A. Strong*

Those of us who teach American politics and struggle each semester to find the right books and articles to assign to our students often ignore the larger arena of public education. The truth is, most people do not take our courses. And most citizens get their information about politics and political institutions from the media and from the books written by authors who get interviewed on the Phil Donahue Show. The distance between political education in the classroom and in the living room is often great, and is certainly so in the case of the American presidency. What we teach about presidents and the White House may be important, but what the public learns from more pervasive sources is more likely to have an effect on the state of the nation.

In the decade following Vietnam and Watergate, public perceptions of presidents and the presidency have been erratic. We have welcomed new chief executives, some of whom came to office from outside the mainstream of Washington politics; we have hoped for their success; and we have relatively quickly lost confidence in them. In 1976 and 1980 both Presidents Ford and Carter had to fight for the nomination of their own party, despite all the advantages that supposedly accompany incumbency. Though both were able to win nomination, both lost in subsequent general elections. Ronald Reagan has recently won a dramatic reelection victory, but at 74 he is already the oldest individual to hold that office. No president has served for a full two terms since Dwight Eisenhower; and one-term presidencies, which were typical in the decades before the Civil War and at the end of the 19th century, may become the norm for the remainder of this century.

*Reprinted with the permission of
Teaching Political Science, published by
Heldref Publications,
4000 Albemarle St., N.W.,
Washington, DC 20016.

The reasons for this phenomenon are well known to political scientists. There has been a general decline in public respect for politicians and political institutions as a result of the war in Southeast Asia and the scandals of the Nixon era. Incumbency may no longer be an automatic advantage in presidential elections. Significant changes in the presidential selection system may have made it easier to challenge a sitting president and to win the nomination without being well known in the party. Furthermore, new and complicated issues on the domestic and international agenda have made it difficult for any president to manage the economy or foreign policy without taking serious political risks. All of these factors are important, but the pattern of enthusiastically greeting new leaders and then gradually destroying them may also be a product of the way most Americans learn about politics. The way the public reads, or misreads, presidents may contribute to the long term instability of the modern presidency.

We first meet prospective presidents in the course of a campaign that now begins well over a year before the New Hampshire primary. The field of candidates is always large, especially in the party out of office; and media coverage is, at best, superficial. The importance of early caucuses and primaries and the limits on what can be spent in those contests, forces candidates to schedule as much time as possible meeting the voters in those parts of the country that by accident or tradition have become barometers of campaign progress. Most of us, who do not live in Iowa or New Hampshire, never see candidates in person. All we know is what we read in print or see on television. One prominent Democrat who chose not to run for the presidency in 1976 (and there were not many who made that choice) lamented that "a candidacy today triggers a thousand skirmishes, a welter of endless draining detail. It plunges the candidate into a morass of unintelligible regulations and dervish-like activity all largely beyond his control and comprehension." With an oversized field, "the press is beleaguered and spread too thin. Commentators gauge the viability of candidates by the most superficial devises: the size of campaign bankrolls or the volume of applause at joint appearances." Television, he said, "offers episodes and spectacles, and the citizen is hard put to fathom their significance" (Stevenson 1977, 190).

Media coverage does not improve as the field narrows. The primary season is covered like a professional sport with interrupted prime time programming, instant commentary, and emphasis on the current standings in polls and surveys. Actual victories in primary elections may, or may not, be important depending on media generated expectations. Lyndon Johnson, not Eugene McCarthy, won the New Hampshire primary in 1968, and John Anderson somehow turned a second place finish in the Massachusetts primary into a national political party. Both McCarthy and Anderson did better than expected and were rewarded with media attention. That attention is, of course, a mixed blessing since the members of the press and the network reporters who descend on a success- ful candidate are competing for headlines and a few precious minutes on the evening news. As a result, trivial comments or events may become major news stories as happened with Edmund Muskie's public tears, George Romney's "brainwashing," Jimmy Carter's "ethnic purity," and a joke of questionable taste told by Ronald Reagan during the 1980 campaign within earshot of an ambitious journalist. Fear of gaffes and the disproportionate coverage they receive encourages some campaign managers carefully to control access to their candidates and to present them to the public in elaborately planned events or paid commercial advertising. The combination of eager journalists and cautious managers distorts the lessons learned about a prospective president during the course of a campaign. Even when we get to see candidates in so called debates, we often learn little from them. The numerous candidate con- frontations in the last two presidential campaigns have produced only two contributions to our political language: "There he goes again," and "Where's the beef?" Future historians reading these phrases out of con- text will be hard pressed to explain their significance. The substance of issues and the character of candidates can get lost in the search for winners and signs of their weakness conducted by the media, in the banality of candidate debates, and in the production of an image manufactured by a campaign staff.

When the campaign ends, the victor is often an individual not well known to the nation that elected him. Ironically, this ignorance seems to generate enthusiasm rather than skepticism. The basic optimism of Americans, the horse race coverage of the election, and the promises that naturally accumulate during a long campaign, all contribute to heightened public expectations. So does the first generation of books about the new president.

Among the journalists who travel the campaign trail, there are always a few would-be Theodore Whites planning to write the definitive descrip- tion of the making of whomever becomes president. Where the daily campaign reporting can trivialize an election, these books glorify it, depicting the successful candidate and his advisers as brilliant strategists and connecting the election results to the mood of the nation and the fate of the planet. The typical book in this category tells us little about how the president was made and often borrows from the biographical material produced by the candidate and his organization. They repeat and refine the campaign image suggesting that anyone capable of winning something as mysterious as a presidential election will have little trouble ruling the nation. Unfortunately, it is not that simple.

Because expectations are high and because the popularity of even narrowly elected presidents soars with inauguration, new administrations are tempted to do as much as possible in their first one hundred days. During the period, the leading members of the administration do not yet know each other; their bureaucratic battles over White House turf and presidential access are intense; and their desire to carry out the president's mandate often blinds them to the fact that the Congress may have gotten a very different mandate from the same election. Making decisions early in a presidency is always difficult; sometimes it is disastrous. The Bay of Pigs, the Nixon pardon, the WIN program, the cancellation of "wasteful" water projects, and the tax legislation of 1981 all occurred early in recent administrations and are regarded as errors in policy or political judgment by at least some of those involved. Such errors inaugurate a new state in presidential reporting. The media resources that are spread too thin during a presidential campaign are fully focused on the White House and Washington as soon as the campaign is over. Sometime in the first year of a presidency the press, which excessively praised the election victor, begins to attack the office incumbent. Fueled by leaks that sometimes produce inaccurate stories, and almost always produce biased ones, the media dissects an administration searching for the rise and fall of presidential advisers and the winners and losers in internal policy disputes. Even if there is relative harmony between White House and cabinet and within the president's staff, a subtle media assault continues. Every new economic statistic or foreign fiasco is reported from the lawn of the presidential residence, even if it has little to do with the policies of the administration. If the news is bad, as it often is, the president is somehow to blame. If the news is good, political manipulation may be implied. The daily coverage of the White House press corps gradually erodes the standing of a new president. Meanwhile, commentators seek to put a stamp on the new administration and investigative journalists, with rakes at the ready, take up the search for muck. All of this increases the importance of early performance and virtually insures that something scandalous about the president, his family, or his appointees will be discovered.

The Carter administration provides an excellent example of what the commentators and muckrakers do to a presidency. Though both groups had a lot to say about the Carter White House, they never managed to give us a clear or consistent picture of that administration. When the President walked down Pennsylvania Avenue, wore a sweater during a fireside chat, left Washington for a town meeting in New England, and answered citizen's questions on national television, he was accused of being all style and no substance. As the administration developed, it became clear that the President was pursuing a variety of substantive domestic and international policies, including many that were unpopular. Carter, the careful image cultivator, became Carter, the naive and idealistic engineer, ignorant of the ways of Washington and destined to fail. Later, when he began to set priorities for his legislative program, change tactics on controversial issues, and compromise with the Congress, he was protrayed as indecisive. By the time he had defeated Edward Kennedy for the 1980 nomination, he was once again described as a consummate politician willing to manipulate anything, including the hostage crisis, in order to achieve reelection. There may be some truth in each of these glimpses into the Carter White House, but together they constitute a strange package of contradictory assessments where the whole is considerably less than the sum of the parts.

While the commentators were trying, without much success, to label Carter and his administration, the investigative journalists were unlocking a series of minor "...gates" concerning the banking practices of Bert Lance, the social graces and alledged drug use of Hamilton Jordan, the bizarre financial and diplomatic dealings of brother Billy, and the suspected campaign contributions of the family peanut business. Though none of these investigations ever led to a successful prosecution, and some were clearly based on frivolous evidence, they were all given exhaustive media coverage. Admittedly, the significance of these events was exacerbated by a President who had been almost sanctimonious in his campaign against the excesses of Watergate and who remained loyal to close advisers even when that loyalty involved obvious political costs. But neither of these factors fully explains the attention given to the relatively minor scandals of the Carter administration. Reagan has received much the same treatment though his personal popularity has not suffered from the allegations and revelations about his cabinet officers and personal staff. After several years in office, all recent presidents have complained about media reporting that ignored the substance of their policies in favor of the play of personalities and the possibilities of wrong-doing.

The books and articles written about a president at midterm are usually the work of Washington journalists or administration dropouts. Though some of these, like James Fallow's articles on Carter or Lou Cannon's biography of Reagan, are serious attempts to help us understand the occupant of the oval office, most are merely repetitions of accumulated media commentary and expose (Fallows 1979, 243-244). At least one of these books is subtitled, "The Man and the Myth," and tells us the shocking truth that the real president is not what his campaign advertising led us to expect. These books become plentiful just as the extended election season begins anew, producing a new cycle of challengers and campaign coverage.

If much of what is written about a sitting president is limited by contradictory commentary and a taste for scandal, the first batch of administration memoirs, which appear shortly after a president leaves office, do little to elevate public perception. In part, this is because they tend to become an apologia for the allegations that surround the author and the president he served. At their best, as in Henry Kissinger's monumental memoirs (the length reflects the number of accusations Kissinger must answer), they provide a detailed defense of the decisions that were made, along with personality sketches of the leading administration members and speculation about how history will treat their time in office. The style and scope of Kissinger's work is, however, unusual. Most political memoirs are more mundane. They add new tidbits to old media stories and provide pieces for the puzzle of presidential personality. Some disguise as much as they reveal. This is partly because their tone is defensive, but it is also because it is difficult to be honest about recent experiences in high office. Some former officials have future ambitions; others are emotionally exhausted. The intensity of working near the top of the executive branch and the sudden loss of its powers and perks can lead to a period of decompression, and even depression. That period may last for years. George Reedy, one of Lyndon Johnson's press secretaries, did not write a revealing account of his service to Johnson until 1982 (Reedy, 1982). No one has yet done so for Gerald Ford or Jimmy Carter.

Presidential memoirs, with the possible exception of those written by Ulysses S. Grant, are uniformly disappointing.[1] It is rare to have a successful politician who is also a skillful writer, and the authorship of some presidential books is suspect. When it is clear that memoirs were actually written by the former president, as is the case with Jimmy Carter and Richard Nixon, the revelations they contain are often indirect. Carter tells us much about foreign affairs, provides a lively account of the Camp David negotiations, but says little about the Democratic Party, the Congress, or domestic politics. He describes his early months in office as a "graduate course in America" as if being president was a matter of mastering a field of study rather than building political coalitions (1982). Those who regarded Carter as a smiling creator of a clever political image will be surprised by the extent to which his book deals almost exclusively with the substance of policy. Those substantive discussions can be fascinating, but the more important aspects of his administration may be the ones he does not discuss. Nixon's memoirs are a long and rambling review of his political career (1978). They move abruptly from strategic speculations, to partisan political statements, to dubious policy defenses, to passages of warm personal observations that are somehow both genuine and awkward. The structure of the book, more than its substance, may give us insight into one of the most complex and perplexing individuals to occupy the White House. But the insight is limited. According to the biography of Fawn Brodie, Nixon was an habitual liar; he may also have been a master of self-deception (1981). The real Richard Nixon remains elusive.

It should not be surprising that the instant history provided by administration memoirs is not much better than the instant commentary provided by the media. Balance and perspective are qualities we expect to emerge from the passage of time and the efforts of historians. Respect for the Truman presidency has steadily increased in the last few decades and scholarship on the Eisenhower administration is currently undergoing major revisions. After thirty years Truman looks better to citizens who now appreciate the hazards of world leadership and respect the decisiveness of his responses to early Cold War crises. Dwight Eisenhower's reputation has improved with the release of his private diaries and papers that show a more active and effective chief executive than was ever previously suspected.[2] Future historians will no doubt revise the public judgements of recent presidents, but their work will be increasingly difficult.

The volume of presidential papers has grown enormously over the last several presidencies. Much of it is of dubious value. Henry Kissinger warns, in the introduction to his *White House Years*, that the documents associated with a presidential decision are likely to confuse future scholars. Presidential advisers do not put their real opinions on paper, not knowing who will read, or xerox, or leak the memorandums they write. "Contemporary practices of unauthorized or liberalized disclosure," Kissinger explains, "come close to ensuring that every document is written with an eye to self-protection. The journalist's gain is the historian's loss" (1979, 22). Another problem may be the existence of presidential libraries, and the administration of their holdings by archivists appointed by the president and his family. George Reedy refers to the Johnson Library as a mausoleum built to preserve an image of Johnson, that is incomplete, if not altogether false. Robert Caro, in the first volume of his biography of Johnson, reports that the oral history interviews on deposit in the Johnson Library all describe LBJ as an amiable and ambitious college student. Caro's own account of Johnson's years at San Marcos State Teachers College reveal an insecure young man who was obsequious to his elders and obnoxious to his fellow students, a chronic braggart whose nickname was "Bull" (1982, vol. 1, chap 8, 141-60). In Caro's work, the product of seven years of research and hundreds of interviews, we are just beginning to see evidence of Johnson's character that was omitted or distorted in earlier accounts.

Why does it take so long to get even close to understanding a president? Some of the fault belongs to the media, some to presidents, and a good deal of it belongs to each of us. Journalism, as a profession, is no worse than any other; and the best journalists would compare favorably with successful politicians or academics. Nevertheless, the media regularly gives us a distorted picture of presidents and the presidency. They spend too much time on the White House lawn, and pay too much attention to the gossip that leaks, and sometimes pours, from the corridors of power. They focus on personalities at the expense of substance and seem to have an unquenchable thirst for scandal. Furthermore, though they attempt to be passive and objective observers, it is almost impossible for them to do so. In a society in which individual voters increasingly make their own political judgments without the help of ward committeemen, or shop stewards, or traditional party affiliations, the dispensing of information and the shaping of opinion have become vital commodities in every political contest. More by default than design, the media has become the principal mediator of power in presidential politics. With the decline of political parties, it is press and television coverage, rather than the endorsements of bosses and notables, that wins primaries and nominations. When elections are over, it is the media that makes the initial and crucial evaluations of performance in office.

This growing power of the media has had a corrupting effect on candidates and incumbents who too often practice sycophancy and sophistry for the benefit of their media judges. Seymour Hersh reports that at the height of Henry Kissinger's power and prestige, he spent at least half his time dealing with reporters and columnists (1983, 204). Whether one is a devotee or a detractor of the former Secretary of State, it is important to note the time and energy he devoted to press relations. It is an increasingly serious issue whether success in policymaking is a matter of substantive solutions or media management. Presidential assistants from recent administrations uniformly complain that the day's agenda in the White House is established by the front pages, editorial commentary, and network coverage of the major news organizations. This means that the current crisis, no matter how minor, always overshadows the long-term problem, no matter how serious. The White House staff becomes adept at answering allegations rather than planning strategies, and is tempted to manage the news rather than run the government. At its worst in the Nixon administration, when many of the president's senior advisers were former public relations executives, this fixation with controlling the media produced shallow advisers and morally dubious behavior. But even in less paranoid presidencies, the problem remains. When the press honestly tries to report the truth and White House press secretaries earnestly try to get their message across, the two clash in inevitable accusations of bias and manipulation. Both faults are almost always present to some degree, and the combination produces a public cynicism that is independent of memories of Watergate. That cyncism is rapidly becoming a permanent feature of American politics and a serious road-block to any balanced perception of the presidency.

A free and commercial press, like an open and democratic society, should not be evaluated without reference to its public and their character. American news organizations are highly competitive and un-usually responsive to their audience. If political reporting is superficial, if it emphasizes personalities and tantilizes with hints of impropriety, it may be that this is what most of us want. A nation that idolizes in-dividualism and creates temporary celebrities in almost every field is likely to make heroes out of newly elected leaders. Those same leaders will quickly fall and lose our trust, not because we have a sense of tragedy, but because we have a passion for soap opera and an impatience with things as they are. American character may be at the heart of our perceptions, and misperceptions, of political leaders and institutions. On the whole, Americans have never been very realistic about presidents. We invented stories about Washington and Lincoln when the truth about their youth was unknown or uninteresting. In the 19th century, we were often attracted to catchy campaign slogans or false claims regarding log cabin births, and to some extent, we have always conducted presidential elections as if they were a combination of a beauty pageant and a medicine show. But if misunderstanding presidents is an American tradi-tion, it is also one that is getting worse.

The presidency since Franklin Delano Roosevelt has become a more powerful and important institution, the hub of an expanded federal govern-ment that constantly touches our lives, and the most powerful office in the western world. We now have added reasons to care about who occupies the oval office and what is done there. More importantly, in the last few decades we have convinced ourselves that we know our presidents far better than in fact we do. Politics in the age of television created an illusion of intimacy and a false familiarity that makes it easy to mistake media image for presidential character. When we think we know our leaders, we tend to become all the more disillusioned when we dis-cover that they are not what we expect. We put ourselves through a cycle of enthusiasm and disappointment that is damaging to the strength and stability of our political system.

That cycle may well be about to begin. Ronald Reagan has won a decisive reelection, but he faces serious problems in domestic and foreign policy. If his budget and tax proposals become stalemated in congress, if the economy takes a turn for the worse, and if arms control negotiations fail to produce progress toward agreements, Reagan's loyal supporters may suddenly abandon him. Such a public response might, in fact, be justified by events, but it might also be a reflection of what the American public knows, or thinks it knows, about his president and the presidency. Political leadership in the last fifteen years of this century is bound to be difficult, it will probably be made more so by what our citizens usually learn about politicians and political institutions.

NOTES

1. And Grant's memoirs do not, of course, cover his years in the White House.
2. See especially, Fred I. Greenstein. 1982. *The Hidden-Hand Presidency.* New York: Basic Books.

REFERENCES

Brodie, Fawn. 1981. *Richard Nixon, The Shaping of His Character.* New York: Norton.

Caro, Robert A. 1982. *The Years of Lyndon Johnson, Vol. I.* New York: Knopf.

Carter, Jimmy. 1982. *Keeping Faith.* New York: Bantam Books.

Fallows, James. 1979. The Passionless Presidency. *Atlantic.* (May and June).

Cannon, Lou. 1982. *Reagan.* New York: Putnam.

Hersh, Seymour. 1983. *The Price of Power.* New York: Summit Books.

Kissinger, Henry. 1979. *The White House Years.* Boston: Little Brown.

Nixon, Richard. 1978. *RN.* New York: Grosset & Dunlap.

Reedy, George. 1982. *Lyndon B. Johnson, A Memoir.* New York: Andrews and McMeel.

Stevenson, Adlai III. 1977. In Jules Witcover, *Marathon.* New York: Viking

Gorbachev and the Challenge of Reform: Stirrings in the Soviet System?
Nicolai N. Petro

Most observers of the Soviet Union can easily agree that the current leading indicators of the health of the Soviet economy and society point to the need for serious reforms. They are often profoundly pessimistic, however, about whether such changes can be effected.

One group of scholars perceives the population as impotent stoics who, after the horrors of the Stalin years, will tolerate pretty much anything. Another group, while more sanguine about the popular desire for reforms, sees them as largely irrelevant to the political process. They see the Party leadership, which could effect reforms, as interested solely in preserving the status quo. Pessimism about prospects for fundamental reform under the current regime is thus the common denominator of most Soviet watchers.

The premise of this essay is that recent development in Soviet society among the top leadership, the middle level technical intelligentsia, and the populace, if taken together, offer a possibility for bridging the existing chasm between rulers and ruled in the USSR. The impetus for a common orientation toward change is now universally recognized need for consequential reform of the economic system.

The first event of significance is the emergence of a young and vigorous new Soviet leader, Mikhail S. Gorbachev. His first mark of distinction is that he has become the most candid prominent critic of economic and social conditions in the country to emerge in twenty years. His criticisms are reminiscent of Nikita Khrushchev's blistering revelations about the state of Soviet agriculture after Stalin's death, because for the first time since Khrushchev a Soviet leader has placed the blame for this condition upon faulty planning, lack of proper incentives, and failure to encourage private plot farming.[1]

Similarly, Gorbachev has been an outspoken critic of the state of the Soviet economy from the outset. Archie Brown has observed that his favorite words when speaking publicly about the need for changes in the economy seem to be "space" [prostor], "innovative" [novatorskii], and "self-management" or "self-government" [samoupravlenie].[2] Another frequent word is "crisis," which he uses to describe the present state of society at large, not just the economy.[3]

But is Gorbachev truly interested in reform, and even if he is, does it matter? Close biographical studies, when taken in conjunction with numerous testimonies of individuals now living in the West who knew Gorbachev as a student or as a minor Party official all seem to concur that Gorbachev himself is indeed what he appears to be — i.e., interested in substantive reforms. He was apparently an exceptional student who went out of his way to do additional independent study. In college he was certainly not enamored of and at times was even openly critical of Stalinist propaganda.[4]

As First Secretary of the Stavropol' regional party organization, from whence he went directly to Moscow, he advocated the "family-based production system" [zvenevaia sistema], even after the Party had officially condemned it as an attempt to restore capitalism. He resurrected the idea, now a prominent feature of the Chinese agricultural resurgence, as Central Committee Secretary responsible for agriculture in March 1983.

Since his arrival in Moscow, rumors have abounded about his "progressive" and "reformist" attitudes. One of the most persistent was that he made his subordinates read the agricultural reform program of Arkady Stolypin, Tsar Nicholas II's prime minister (1906-11). Also, he was said to favor the more liberal Hungarian economic model, and wish for a stricter adherence to "socialist legality."[5]

But even if it were true that Gorbachev the individual desires such reforms, the question remains, is there anything Gorbachev, the Central Committee's General Secretary, can do about it? As the chief party official his options for reform appear sparse indeed. There is every indication that the present majority in the Politburo, essentially the same as that under Brezhnev, is totally uninterested in change. The election of Chernenko to succeed Andropov, as well as the fact that Gorbachev's own appointment was less than unanimous, can be taken as an indication of the hesitancy with which the ruling majority supports him.[6]

It is scarcely surprising, therefore, that, judging from the report of the first Politburo meeting after Chernenko's funeral, Gorbachev was given a very narrowly defined mandate, one that does not even contemplate the possibility of moving away from the status quo.[7] There is every indication that Gorbachev was hired to look after the collective interests of the leadership, certainly not to strike out on his own course. And when one looks at his policies and contrasts them to his rhetoric, it is hard not to agree with Alexander Shtromas that although "the style is vigorous, enthusiastic, creating the impression that from this time on everything will be very different from what it used to be; the substance is, however, not much else than a vigorous restatement of past policies."[8]

Hence, the considerable confusion and disagreement today not only about what exactly Gorbachev would like to do, but also about whether he will be able to do it. A resolution of these issues will have to wait until next February when it will be revealed at the XXVII Party Congress to what extent Gorbachev has been able to pack this body with his own spokesmen, and thus redefine his original mandate. So far, he appears to be well on the way toward asserting firm control and, if he succeeds, one can only agree with Archie Brown that those who "think...that he will be hamstrung, may be in for a surprise."[9]

The western public's attention of late has been focused almost exclusively on the top echelon of the Soviet leadership. A change of such significance naturally tends to focus one's attention. It is important to bear in mind, however, that whatever changes are proposed will succeed or fail largely to the degree to which they respond to the desires expressed by various other levels of Soviet society. Two groups can be expected to play an increasingly significant role in the country's future, if the path of reform is chosen.

The first group might be called the disaffected technological intelligentsia. The origins of the dissident movement among disaffected intellectuals has been widely discussed.[10] Dissidents, however, as a rule eschewed the official channels of power although they often appealed to the government for recognition. There now seem to be a number of prominent intellectuals tackling the issue of reform within official channels and meeting with some success.[11] The most notable has been achieved by Tatyana I. Zaslavskaya, director of the Institute of Economics and the Organization of Industrial Production of the Siberian section of the Academy of Sciences. Zaslavskaya is the author of a memorandum on the state of the economy and its effect on production and social relations presented at a restricted conference of leading economists, social scientists, and administrators in 1983. The so-called "Novosibirsk Memorandum," representing the joint efforts of the Academy, is a scathing indictment of the factors behind lagging production, lack of international competitiveness of Soviet goods, and political corruption. Though couched in Marxist terms, the document places the blame for these ills squarely upon centralized planning and argues ominously that without serious reforms, "the system of productive relations, and hence the mechanisms of the state's management of the economy...[are falling] behind the level of development of productive forces," the classic marxian recipe for a revolutionary situation.[12]

The document was commissioned by the ailing Andropov, but its conclusions were rejected by a plenary session of the General Committee. After the head of the Siberian section, academician Abel Aganbegyan, was reprimanded, the document was leaked to *Washington Post* correspondent Dusko Dodder and found its way onto the front pages of major western newspapers.

After a two year absence, Zaslavskaya made a dramatic reappearance just this summer in a lengthy interview published in the government newspaper *Izvestiia*. In this interview she is given the opportunity to restate publicly her criticisms of lack of adequate economic incentives. Her studies indicate that 90% of workers and 84% of managers [rukovoditeli] feel that under different economic and organizational conditions they could work much more effectively.[13] The choices that need to be made are clear and the overall concept, she says, is agreed upon. The crucial phase now is which strategy to pursue to get around the inevitable opposition of party and bureaucratic hacks.

The implications of Zaslavskaya's case seem to be that for once a member of the disaffected technological intelligentsia, with clear ideas for economic reform, has gotten a boost by the new leadership. As a result, many economic reformers expect to occupy positions of prominence under Gorbachev and are getting ready for a long and bloody fight with the bureaucracy.

The second emergent factor, to which many of the above reformers have pointedly referred, is the renewed potential for popular unrest. Concommitant with the increase in popular discontent is the resurgence of interest in non-official nationalist and religious sentiment. The argument economic reformers make to the party leadership (and which is apparently also taken up by Gorbachev) is that a catastrophe faces the present system unless the issues that have been ignored for the past twenty years are addressed soon. The issue at hand is not merely the "scientific-technological gap" which the Soviet Union faces if it cannot enter the computer age, but the much more fundamental implication of the poor performance of socialist economies as revealed statistically by a variety of official sources. As often happens in Russian history these issues were first raised and popularized in literature, especially in the works of the "village writers" who have criticized the economic and social effects of collectivization on the country, thus calling into question the entire rationale for forced industrialization and centralized economic planning.

What are some of these statistics? Economically, during the period after Stalin's death and through the reign of Khrushchev, increases in real income averaged 3.2% per annum. But according to Zaslavskaya, "in the past 12-15 years a tendency towards a noticeable decline in the rate of growth of the national income began to make itself felt in the development of the economy of the USSR. If in the eighth five-year plan the average annual increase was 7.5 per cent and in the ninth it was 5.8 per cent, then in the tenth it fell to 3.8 per cent, and the first years of the eleventh it was about 2.5 per cent (with the average population growth at 0.8 per cent per annum). This does not provide for either the rate of growth in living standards that is required for the people, or for the intensive technical retooling of production."[14]

Since 1978 it has been estimated that the economy has remained stagnant in all major sectors. In addition, four successive harvest failures between 1979 and 1982 led to the introduction of rationing cards in twenty major cities, for the first time since World War II.[15]

The social effects of massive dysfunction of the economy as also manifest. The most obvious is pervasive alcoholism. In 1978 in the USSR there were one hundred times more deaths attributed to alcohol poisoning than in the US in the same period.[16] Even in areas where the Soviet government has pointed with pride, such as health care, there has been a sharp decline. The crude death rate among the population, which had fallen to 6.9 per thousand by 1964 has been rising steadily since, and was at 10.3 per thousand in 1980. Infant mortality today is three times that of the United States. Whereas other industrialized countries have been making strides in extending life expectancy, in the Soviet Union male life expectancy has dropped from a high 66 years back to 62 today, contributing to a significant rise in one-parent families.[17] The high incidence of abortion (the average Soviet woman undergoes 3-4 abortions in a lifetime compared with 0.75 in the United States), along with abysmal housing conditions (20% of families continue to share single-family apartments with two or more families) have contributed to a dangerously low birthrate among Slavs.[18]

It is not at all surprising, therefore, that reports of discontent and popular pessimism, fear for the future, fear of war, are increasing in frequency, and that discontent is occasionally manifested in public demonstrations against the authorities.

Soviet leaders well recall that in 1962 when Nikita Khrushchev decided to improve the chances for his economic program by raising prices 20-30% in staple goods, the citizens of the city of Novocherkassk occupied and sacked the local Party headquarters and had to be subdued by special military units,[19] and that this was not an isolated instance. Disapproval was manifested publicly, sometimes violently in Kaunas, Moscow, Leningrad, Baku, as well as in the Ukraine, Uzbekistan and Kazakhstan.

In May 1980 history seemed to be repeating itself when 70,000 workers of the Lada automobile plant in Togliatti struck for two days over food shortages in their city. Similarly motivated strikes were noted in their city. Similarly motivated strikes were noted in the city of Gorky, at the Kama river truck plant in Brezhnev, at the tractor plant in Cherkassy and in Estonia. The appearance and temporary successes of Polish Solidarity led to further unrest among workers in 1981: in March at the Donetsk coal mines, in March through June in Kiev, and in the city of Ordzhonikidze in October.

The decade of the eighties marks the emergence of what the Soviet regime fears most — a politically oriented worker's movement. The first attempt to form an independent trade union in the USSR was made by Vladimir Klebanov and six others in 1977. By January of 1978 the group claimed over two hundred members in over one hundred regions of the country. The regime, however, acted quickly to arrest these members. A second effort, known as SMOT (Free Inter-professional Association of Workers) was launched that same year and survived for nearly five years thanks to its semi-conspiratorial procedures. During this time the group disseminated 36 issues of its *Bulletin* with detailed information on working conditions throughout the country. This group was finally suppressed by the arrest of the members of its executive committee; at that time it was also revealed that at least two of the committee's five members espoused distinct political and nationalistic concerns. In his final statement (June 16, 1982) before his arrest Rostislav Evdokimov explained why he joined SMOT:[20]

> First — patriotism.
>
> Second — a clearly defined national self-awareness that is friendly toward the national sentiments of other nations.
>
> Third — religiosity without fanaticism.
>
> Fourth — a striving to achieve for our poeple political, economic, religious and cultural freedoms in their universal and traditional sense, and not as explained to us by communist demagogues.
>
> Fifth — a respect for each individual human person and for the human dignity of nations.
>
> Sixth — striving to avoid any actions of violence, an attempt to devise some political form of national reconciliation, and the rejection of terrorism.

A question that must be on the minds of Soviet leaders is what might occur if the present period of economic stagnation continues or worsens (as many western experts predict)? The argument for reform from above, before it is force upon them from below by a politicization of worker's unrest, might be a compelling one to some in the top leadership.

The purpose of this discussion has not been to argue for the inevitability or even the likelihood of change. That will depend upon a wide variety of factors and upon events which are unpredicatable. It does, however, attempt to belie a popular image of Soviet society as dormant, and try to point out some occurrences meriting broader attention which are occurring at every level of society, not just at the top.

The apparent reliance of some members of each category of society upon the other in arguing for change indicates a cognizance that it is extremely unlikely that any single group of people within the country, including even the Politburo itself, will be able to generate enough impetus to move the Soviet system along the path of domestic reforms. It also indicates perhaps a recognition that popular opinion will play a key role in the success or failure of future economic programs, for in order to be successful reforms must appeal to the desires of individuals and families for a better life. Attempts simply to admonish or penalize workers for pursuing their own interests against those of the State will, as Andropov's aborted attempt shows, inevitably fail.

The Party leadership, however, is also constrained by its own perception that truly popular reforms would undermine not only the actual practice, but also the philosophical rationale for communist rule. Yet, without such reforms, many observers both inside and outside the country predict that the regime will become increasingly impoverished, backward, corrupt, and repressive. Without reforms, also, the danger that popular discontent with declining living standards might explode into violence against the regime becomes more acute — especially if no hope for improvement is offered. It is not surprising therefore to find many in the Soviet Union, both among the elite and the populace, relieved that there is now a leader who actually appears willing to lead. The real tests of Gorbachev's leadership have yet to come, however. The next few years should be very interesting ones for observers of the Soviet Union, although it is not certain whether for Soviet citizens, living in such interesting times will be a blessing or a curse.

NOTES

1. See the discussion of Khrushchev's economic policies in Basil Dmytryshyn *USSR*, fourth ed. (New York: Scribner's, 1984), 279-86.
2. "Korennoi vopros ekonomischeskoi politiki partii," *Pravada*, June 12, 1985, 2.

3. See, for example, Gorbachev's speeches to a meeting in the Central Committee dedicated to the quickening of scientific-technological progress cited above. The full is available in *Soviet Media Daily Digest*, # 292 (June 14, 1985). Also his speech to gathering of Leningrad Party activists "*Soedinenie nauki c proizvodstvom — velenie vremeni*" in *Soviet Media Daily Digest*, # 249 (May 22, 1985).
4. Among the personal reminiscences about Gorbachev, see Zdenek Mlynarz, "Il mio compagno di studi Mikhail Gorbachev," *L'Unita* (April 19, 1985), 9; and a round-table discussion "Vashe mnenie o novom genseke" in issues four and five (April and May, 1985) in *Possev*.
5. See, for example, evidence cited by Archie Brown and Michael Kaser, eds., in *Soviet Policy for the 1980s* (London: Basingstoke & Macmillan, 1982), 102, 241-45; and Archie Brown, "Gorbachev: New Man in the Kremlin," in *Problems of Communism*, vol. 34, # 3 (May-June 1985), 1-23.
6. The notice of the Central Committee's Plenary session published in *Pravda* (March 12, 1985) refers to his election as *edinodushno* [by consensus] rather than as *edinoglasno* [unanimously].
7. See, "V Politburo TsK KPSS," *Pravda* (March 22, 1985), 1.
8. Alexander Shtromas, "How the End of the Soviet System May Come About," a paper presented to the Second International Congress of Professor's World Peace Academy, Geneva, Switzerland (August 13-18, 1985), 36-37.
9. Archie Brown, "Can Gorbachev Make a Difference?" *Detente*, # 3 (May 1985), 7.
10. See, for example, the recent work by Ludmilla Alexeyeva, *Soviet Dissent* (Middletown, CT: Wesleyan U., 1985).
11. Among the most prominent among economists are Abel Aganbegyan, Evgenii Ambartsumov, Fedor Burlatsky, Anatolii Butenko, Boris Kurashvili, and, of course, Tatiana Zaslavskaya.
12. The full text of the Novosibirsk document is in Radio Liberty's *Arkhiv Samizdata* (# 5042). An English translation is available in *Survey* Vol. 28, No. 1 (Spring 1984), 88.
13. Tatiana Zaslavskaya, "Vybor strategii" [an interview in] *Izvestiia*, (June 1, 1985), 3.
14. *Survey*, op. cit., 88.
15. See Murray Feshbach, *The Soviet Union*, A Publication of the Population Reference Bureau, Inc., XXXVII, No. 3, (August 1982), 9; John P. Hardt ed. *Soviet Economy in the 1980s* (Selected Papers submitted to the Joint Economic Committee, U.S. Congress, December 31, 1982), 367-68, 370, 372, 383; "Soviets Call Grain Crisis Acute," *Detroit Free Press* (October 23, 1984), 7A.
16. Feshbach, *The Soviet Union*, 35; Cullen Murphy, "Watching the Russians," *Atlantic Monthly* (February 1983), 33-52; Peter Wiles, "The Worsening of Soviet Economic Performance" in Jan Drewnowski ed., *Crisis in the East European Economies* (New York: St. Martin's, 1982), 152.
17. Feshbach, op. cit., 30-33
18. Lewis Gann and Mikhail Bernstam, "Will the Soviet Stay Communist?" *The Intercollegiate Review* (Spring/Summer 1984), 13-22

19. Hardt, *Soviet Economy*, 349-66; Marshall Goldman, *USSR in Crisis* (New York: Norton, 1983), 110. A most extensive discussion of worker's unrest in Russia proper is found in *Solidarnost'*, 1980-82: *o rabochem dvizhenii v Pol'she i o rabochem dvizhenii v Rossii*, 2nd ed. (Frankfurt, West Germany: Possev, 1982), 210-97.
20. *Solidarnost'*, op. cit., 295.